THE AWAKENING
OF THE
HUMAN SPIRIT

HAZRAT INAYAT KHAN

OMEGA PRESS
Publisher and Bookseller
New Lebanon

The Awakening of the Human Spirit
©1982 Omega Publications. All rights reserved.
Omega Uniform edition, 1988

Published by:
    OMEGA PUBLICATIONS INC
    256 DARROW ROAD
    NEW LEBANON NY 12125-2615
    www.omegapub.com

Printed in the United States of America.
ISBN 0-930872-35-5
10 9 8 7 6 5 4

CONTENTS

Introduction by Pir Vilayat Inayat Khan vii

1. The Alchemy of Happiness 1
2. Spiritual Attainment: The Aim of Life 7
3. Life's Symphony: The Desire to Live 12
4. The Knowledge of Every Living Soul: The Desire
    for Knowledge 19
5. To Deny Self and Affirm God: The Desire for Power .. 24
6. The Desire for Happiness 28
7. The Desire for Peace 32
8. The Freedom of the Soul I 36
9. The Freedom of the Soul II 46
10. The Freedom of the Soul III 52
11. "Cry Out in the Name of Thy Lord" 58
12. Even in the Breaking of the Heart 72
13. To Hold Love's Flame High 77
14. There Will Come a Day of Awakening 82
15. Except a Man Be Born Again 92
16. The Purpose for Which We Were Born 98
17. There is One Vital Substance 105
18. For the Rosebud to Bloom 112
19. A Light that Will Always Shine 117
20. And He Will No More Find Himself to Be What He
    Thought Himself to Be 124
21. The Lifting of the Veil 132
22. The Inner Life: The Consciousness of Perfection 141
23. Preparing for the Journey 152

24. To Make God a Reality 158

25. The Attainment of the Inner Life 162

26. To Become All Things to All Men 168

27. There is a Spirit of Freedom Hidden Within Man 172

28. The Singer of the Divine Song, The Astrologer of the
    Entire Cosmos 176

29. So the Wise Live Among All the People of This World 180

30. A Living God 185

31. Five Different Kinds of Spiritual Souls 190

32. "I Am the Way and the Truth" 195

33. The Dance of the Soul 201

INTRODUCTION
by
Pir Vilayat Inayat Khan

As a spiritual teacher, Hazrat Inayat Khan was very definitely a spokesman for the present outlook, the new ways of looking at spirituality. Rather than enjoining upon his disciples to leave the world for an inexpressible bliss—at the cost of shirking responsibilities—he showed the way to find a far greater fulfillment: by making our spiritual ideals a reality in our lives, transforming ourselves in our relationship with people and situations.

The teaching here presented describes the sequence of inner stages that the adept goes through in his quest for spiritual realism. First he reconnoiters for his purpose in the life he is involved with, spotlighting any obstacles within himself standing in the way of his fulfillment. Then he launches into the deeper processes. Here he discovers vaster potentialities in his being than he had grasped so far, and consequently discovers the personal aspect of God as being imprinted in his very being, rather than entertaining the abstract notion of God that he had held previously.

In fact he experiences himself as the One Being, having become many. He now envisions what he thought was his experience as being God's experience through him; his thoughts as being God's thoughts through him; his emotions as being divine emotions; and his accomplishment as being God's fulfillment through his hands and feet.

As his consciousness outreaches its previous limited purview, he takes the next step in the human evolutionary process. Hazrat Inayat Khan appears to have been the first to use the phrase "planetary consciousness," way back in 1924. Today, faced with prospects of encounters with extraplanetary intelligences, we are discovering our planetary identity as the human family, the fulfillment of God's purpose.

Such was Hazrat Inayat Khan's message: It is not enough to live in the spirit: what we need today is a human spirit. This is more than a quickening by the action of ineffable spirit. It is the awakening of spirit in the human by lending oneself to the grilling action of truth. At the moment when one has become the truth, one is stirred to the quick by the realization of being the very being of God. This is the ultimate breakthrough. Hazrat Inayat Khan embodies the essence of his teaching in these words: "Make God a reality and He will make you the truth."

That God should reach fulfillment in man rather than man trying to reach up into the unknown, and that man may plug in to so much richness and make it real in himself, that is the thrill in the teaching of Hazrat Inayat Khan.

THE AWAKENING OF THE HUMAN SPIRIT

Chapter 1.

THE ALCHEMY OF HAPPINESS

Happiness is your own being, your own self—that self that is the most precious thing in life.

The soul is called in Sanskrit, in the terms of the Vedanta, *atman,* which means happiness or bliss itself. This does not mean that happiness belongs to the soul; it means that the soul itself is happiness. Today we often confuse happiness with pleasure, but pleasure is only an illusion, a shadow of happiness; and in this delusion man may pass his whole life, seeking after pleasure and never finding satisfaction. There is a Hindu saying that man looks for pleasure and finds pain. Every pleasure seems happiness in outward appearance; it promises happiness, for it is the shadow of happiness. Just as the shadow of a person is not the person, although it represents his form, so pleasure represents happiness, but is not happiness in reality.

According to this idea, one rarely finds souls in this world who know what happiness is; people are constantly disappointed in one thing after another. That is the nature of life

1

in the world. It is so deluding that if man were disappointed a thousand times, he would still take the same path, for he knows no other. The more we study life, the more we realize how rarely there is a soul who can honestly say, "I am happy." Almost every soul, whatever his position in life, will say he is unhappy in some way or another, and if you ask him why, he will probably say that it is because he cannot attain to the position, power, property, possessions, or rank for which he has worked for years. Perhaps he craves money and does not realize that possessions give no satisfaction; perhaps he says he has enemies, or that those whom he loves do not love him. There are a thousand excuses for unhappiness that the reasoning mind will make.

But is even one of these excuses ever entirely correct? Do you think that if these people gained their desires they would be happy? If they possessed all, would that suffice? No, they would still find some excuse for unhappiness; and all the excuses are only like covers over a man's eyes, for deep within is the yearning for the true happiness that none of these things can give. He who is really happy is happy everywhere, in a palace or in a cottage, in riches or in poverty, for he has discovered the fountain of happiness that is situated in his own heart. As long as a person has not found that fountain, nothing will give him real happiness.

The man who does not know the secret of happiness often develops avarice. He wants thousands, and when he gets them they do not satisfy him. He wants millions, and still he is not satisfied; he wants more and more. If you give him your sympathy and service he is still unhappy; even all you possess is not enough, even your love does not help him, for he is seeking in a wrong direction, and life itself becomes a tragedy.

Happiness cannot be bought or sold, nor can you give it to a person who has not got it. Happiness is your own being, your own self—that self that is the most precious thing in life. All religions and all philosophical systems have in different forms taught man how to find it by the religious path or the mystical way; and all the wise ones have in some form or another given a method by which the individual can find that happiness for which the soul is seeking.

Sages and mystics have called this process alchemy. The stories of the Arabian Nights, which symbolize mystical ideas, are full of the belief that there is a philosopher's stone that will turn metals into gold by a chemical process. No doubt this symbolic idea has deluded men in both the East and West; many have thought that a process exists by which gold can be produced. But this is not the idea of the wise; the pursuit of gold is for those who as yet are only children. For those who have the consciousness of reality, gold stands for light or spiritual inspiration. Gold represents the color of light, and therefore an unconscious pursuit after light has made man seek for gold. But there is a great difference between real gold and false. It is the longing for true gold that makes man collect the imitation gold, ignorant that the real gold is within. He satisfies the craving of his soul in this way, as a child satisfies itself by playing with dolls.

This realization is not a matter of age. One man may have reached an advanced age and still be playing with dolls, and his soul may be involved in the search for this imitation gold, while another may have begun in youth to see life in its real aspect. If one studied the transitory nature of life in the world and how changeable it is, and the constant craving of everyone for happiness, one would certainly endeavor at all costs to find something one could depend upon. Man, placed in the midst of this everchanging world, still appreciates and seeks for constancy somewhere. He does not know that he must develop the nature of constancy in himself. It is the nature of the soul to value that which is dependable. But is there anything in the world on which one can depend, which is above change and destruction? All that is born, all that is made, must one day face destruction. All that has a beginning has also an end; but if there is anything one can

depend upon it is hidden in the heart of man. It is the divine
spark, the true philosopher's stone, the real gold, which is
the innermost being of man.

A person may follow a religion and yet not come to the
realization of truth, and of what use is his religion to him if
he is not happy? Religion does not mean depression and
sadness. The spirit of religion should give happiness. God is
happy. He is the perfection of love, harmony, and beauty.
A religious person should be happier than one who is not
religious. If a person who professes religion is always melancholy, his religion is disgraced; the form has been kept, but
the spirit has been lost. If the study of religion and mysticism does not lead to real joy and happiness, it may just as
well not exist, for then it does not help to fulfill the purpose
of life. The world today is sad and suffering as the result of
terrible wars; the religion that answers the demand of life
today is one that invigorates and gives life to souls, that
illuminates the heart of man with the divine light that is
already there; not necessarily by any outer form, though for
some a form may be helpful, but by showing that happiness
that is the desire of every soul.

As for the question of how this method of alchemy is
practiced, the whole process was explained by the alche-
mists in a symbolical way. They said gold is made out of
mercury; the nature of mercury is to be ever-moving, but by
a certain process the mercury is first stilled, and once stilled
it becomes silver; then the silver has to be melted, and the
juice of an herb is poured onto the molten silver, which is
thereby turned into gold. This, of course, gives only an
outline, but one can find detailed explanations of the whole
process. Many childlike souls have tried to make gold by
stilling mercury and melting silver, and they have tried to
find the herb, but they were deluded, and they would have
done better to have worked and earned money.

The real interpretation of this process is that mercury
represents the nature of the ever-restless mind. Especially
when he tries to concentrate, a person realizes that the mind

is ever-restless. The mind is like a restive horse: when it is ridden it is more restive than when it is in the stable. Such is the nature of the mind—it becomes more restless when one desires to control it. It is like mercury, constantly moving.

When by a method of concentration one has mastered the mind, one has taken the first step in the accomplishment of a sacred task. Prayer is concentration, reading is concentration, sitting and relaxing and thinking on one subject are all concentration. All artists, thinkers, and inventors have practiced concentration in some form: they have given their minds to one thing, and by focusing on one object have developed the faculty of concentration, but for stilling the mind a special method taught by the mystic is necessary, just as a singer needs to be taught by a teacher of voice-production.

The secret of this concentration is learned in the science of breath. Breath is the essence of life, the center of life, and the mind may be controlled by a knowledge of the proper method of breathing. For this, instruction from a teacher is a necessity, for since the mystical cult of the East has become known in the West, books have been published, and teaching that had been kept as sacred as religion has been discussed in words, but these can never truly explain the mystery of that which is the center of man's very being. People read these books and begin to play with breath, and often instead of benefiting they injure both mind and body. There are also those who make a business of teaching breathing exercises for money, thus degrading a sacred thing. The science of breath is the greatest mystery there is, and for thousands of years it has been kept as a sacred trust in the schools of the mystics.

When the mind is under perfect control and no longer restless, one can hold a thought at will as long as one wishes. This is the beginning of phenomena. Some abuse these privileges, and by dissipating the power thus obtained, they destroy the silver before turning it into gold. The silver must be heated before it can melt, and with what? With that warmth that is the divine essence in the heart of man, which comes forth as love, tolerance, sympathy, service, humility, and unselfishness, in a stream that rises and falls in a thousand drops, each drop of which could be called a virtue, and all coming from that one stream hidden in the heart of man, the love element; and when it glows in the heart, then the actions, the movements, the tone of the voice, and the expression all show that the heart is warm. The moment this happens a man really lives, he has unsealed the spring of happiness that overcomes all that is jarring and inharmonious, and the spring has established itself as a divine stream.

After the heart is warmed by the divine element, which is love, the next stage is the herb, which is the love of God. But the love of God alone is not sufficient; knowledge of God is also necessary. It is the absence of the knowledge of God that makes a man leave his religion, for there is a limit to man's patience. Knowledge of God strengthens man's belief in God and throws light on the individual and on life. Things become clear; every leaf on a tree becomes as a page of a holy book to one whose eyes are open to the knowledge of God. When the juice of the herb of divine love is poured on the heart, warmed by love for one's fellow men, then that heart becomes the heart of gold, the heart that expresses what God would express. Man has not seen God, but man has then seen God in man, and when this happens, then verily everything that comes from such a man comes from God Himself.

Chapter 2.

SPIRITUAL ATTAINMENT: THE AIM OF LIFE

Spiritual attainment is not only acquired knowledge, it is the soul's appetite.

The main object of life can be only one object, though there may be as many external objects as there are things and beings. There is one object of life for the reason that there is only one life, in spite of the fact that it appears outwardly to be many lives. It is in this thought that we can unite, and it is from this thought that true wisdom is learned. No doubt that main object of life cannot be understood at once, and therefore the best thing for every person is first to pursue his object in life, for in the accomplishment of his personal object he will arrive some day at the accomplishment of that inner object. When man does not understand this, he goes on thinking there is something else to accomplish, and he thinks of all that is before him that is not yet accomplished; that is why he remains a failure.

The person who is not definite about his object has not yet

begun his journey on the path of life. One should therefore first determine one's object for oneself, however small that object is; once it is determined one has begun life. We find with many people that somehow they never happen to find their life's vocation, and what happens then is that in the end they consider their life a failure. All through life, they go from one thing to another, but since they do not know their life's object, they can accomplish very little. When people ask why they do not succeed, the answer is that they have not yet found their object. As soon as a person has found his life's object, he begins to feel at home in this world, where before he had felt himself in a strange world. No sooner has a person found his way than he will prove to be fortunate, because all the things he wants to accomplish will come by themselves. Even if the whole world is against him, he will get such a power that he can hold on to his object against anything. He will acquire such patience that when he is on the way to his object no misfortune will discourage him. There is no doubt that as long as he has not found it he will go from one thing to another, and again to another; and he will think that life is against him. Then he will begin to find fault with individuals, conditions, plans, the climate, with everything. Thus what is called being fortunate or successful is really having the right object. When a person is wearing clothes that were not made for him, he says they are too wide or too short, but when they are his own clothes he feels comfortable in them. Everyone should, therefore, be given freedom to choose his object in life; and if he finds his object, one knows that he is on the right path.

When a person is on the path, there are certain things to be considered. When a person has a knot to unravel and is given a knife to cut it, he has lost a great opportunity in his life. It is a small thing, but by not accomplishing its solution he has gone backward. This is a minor example, but in everything one does, if one has not the patience and confidence to go forward, then one loses a great deal. However small the job a person has undertaken, if he completes it he has accomplished something great. It is not the work that a person has accomplished, it is the very fact of accomplishing that gives him power.

As to what is the main object of every soul, that object may be called spiritual attainment. A person may go through his whole life without it, but there will come a time in his life when although he may not admit it, he will begin to look for it. For spiritual attainment is not only acquired knowledge, it is the soul's appetite; and there will come a day in life when a person will feel the soul's appetite more than any other appetite. No doubt every soul has an unconscious yearning to satisfy the soul's appetite, but at the same time one's absorption in everyday life keeps one so occupied that one has no time to pay attention to it.

The definition of spiritual attainment can be found in the study of human nature. For the nature of man is one and the same, be he spiritual or material. There are five things that man yearns for: life, power, knowledge, happiness, and peace, and the continual appetite that is felt in the deepest self yearns for one or another of these five things.

In order to fulfill the desire to live man eats and drinks and protects himself from all dangers of life; and yet his appetite will never be fully satisfied, because though he may escape all dangers, the last danger, which man calls death, he cannot escape.

In order to obtain power, which is the next thing, a man does everything to gain physical strength, influence, or rank; he seeks every kind of power. And he always runs up against disappointments, because he will find that wherever there is a power of ten degrees, there will always be another power of twenty degrees to run up against. Just think of the great nations whose military power was once so immense that one could never have believed that they would suddenly collapse. One would have thought that it would take them thousands of years to fall, so great was their power. We need not look for it in history, we have just seen this happen in the last few years,* we have only to look at the map.

_____
*In the First World War.

Then there is the desire for knowledge. This desire pro-
motes a tendency to study. A man might study and study
all through his life, but even if he read all the books in all
the great libraries there would still remain the question,
"Why?" That "why" will not be answered by the books he
studies or by exploring the facts that belong to outer life. In
the first place, nature is so profound that man's limited life
is not long enough to probe its depths. Comparatively or
relatively, one may say that one person is more learned than
another, but no one reaches true satisfaction by the outer
study of life.

The fourth kind of appetite is happiness. Man tries to
satisfy it by pleasures, not knowing that the pleasures of this
world cannot make up for the happiness his soul really seeks
after. Man's attempts are in vain; he will find in the end that
every effort he made for pleasure brought greater loss than
gain. Besides, that which is not enduring, which is not real
in its nature, is never satisfactory.

Lastly, there is the appetite for peace. In order to find
peace one leaves the environment that troubles one, one
wants to get away from people, to sit quietly and rest. But
he who is not ready for that peace would not find it even if
he went to the caves of the Himalayas, away from the whole
world.

When considering these five appetites, which are the
deepest man has, one finds that all the efforts man makes to
satisfy them seem to be in vain. They can only be satisfied
by spiritual attainment; that is the only answer to them.

Now the question is how these five things can be gained.
As I have said, the first thing needed is to accomplish the
object that is standing before one immediately: however
small it is, it does not matter. It is by accomplishing it that
one gains power. As one goes further in this way through
one's life, always seeking for the real, one will at the end
come to reality. Truth is attained by the love of truth. When
a person runs away from truth, truth runs away from him.
If he does not run away, then truth is nearer to him than that

which is without truth. There is nothing more precious in life than truth itself; and in loving truth and in attaining to the truth one attains to that religion that is the religion of all churches and of all people. It does not matter then to what church a man belongs, what religion he professes, to what race or nation he belongs; when once he realizes the truth he is all, because he is with all. The obstacle is the disagreement and the misunderstanding before he has attained to the truth. When once he has attained to the truth, there is no more misunderstanding. It is among those who have learned only the outer knowledge that disputes arise, but those who have attained to the truth, whether they come from the North or the South, from whatever country, it does not matter; for when they have understood the truth they are in at-one-ment.

It is this thought that we should keep before us in order to unite the divided sections of humanity, for the real happiness of humanity is in that unity that can be gained by rising above the barriers that divide men.

Chapter 3.

LIFE'S SYMPHONY:
THE DESIRE TO LIVE

*. . . Without doubt this desire of living must be fulfilled.
And the fulfillment of this desire is in getting above the
illusion that is caused by ignorance of the secret of life.*

The desire to live is not only seen among human beings, it
is also seen continually working through the most insignificant little creatures creeping on the earth and living in the
ground. When one sees how even the smallest insect wishes
to avoid any pursuit after it and how it seeks shelter against
any attempt made to touch it, fearing that its life may be
taken away from it, that shows that even the smallest creature in the world, in whom man cannot find a trace of mind,
has a desire to live. It is this desire that, developing in the
lower creation in many and varied aspects, shows in fear, in
the tendency to seek shelter, in the intelligent way of looking around, as the hare does in the fields, and in the deer that
is continually careful to protect itself from other animals.
This desire developed in man shows still greater phenomena

of intelligence. War and peace are brought about by the desire to live: the cause behind war is the desire to live, and the cause of peace is also the desire to live. There is not one normal soul living on earth who has not the desire to live. It is true that a person most distressed, in a mood of unhappiness, will say at the moment, "I would rather not live; I seek death." But this is not the normal condition. One may say, "Why is death not a desirable thing, since it is only a getting rid of the dense body?" But can we not turn the dense body into a light body? Even matter can turn into spirit. If the divine blood begins to circulate through the veins of a person, then this body is no longer a heavy body; it becomes as light as vapor. It is heavy when the weight of the earth has fallen upon it, but when the weight of the earth is taken away from it, it is lighter than the air.

"But," one may say, "is not death an increase of life?" Death is another phase of life. The body is a complete instrument; why should we not make the best of it? Why must one hasten death, if one can be here and do something worthwhile? Sometimes one longs for death because one does not know what one is to do here; one is not yet acquainted with the purpose of life, and it is that which makes one long for death. Every moment in life has its mission; every moment in life is an opportunity. Why should this opportunity be lost? Why not use every moment of one's life towards the accomplishment of that purpose for which we are here? It is a question of bestirring ourselves to make the best use of every moment of life. That itself will give such happiness to a person that he will not wish to go. Even if the angels of death came and were dragging him towards death, he would say, "Let me stay here a while longer; let me finish something that I would like to finish."

That must be the attitude. When a person is in his normal condition of mind, his one desire—his innermost desire—is to live. What does this show? It shows that man has acquired all other desires after coming on earth, but he has brought this desire to live with him to the earth. Only by not understanding the meaning of this desire—its nature and character, its secret—does he submit to its being broken by what is called death, by mortality.

If the desire to live is his innermost desire—if it is a divine substance in him—then there is the answer to this desire also, there is a possibility of the fulfillment of this desire. But when one does not dive deep into the secrets of life, without the knowledge of life and death one becomes subject to disappointment, and that disappointment is death. One may say, "If the desire to live is natural, would it not be better to live and prolong the youthfulness of the body? And how can that be done?" There are three aspects the Hindus have personified, as Brahma, Vishnu, and Maheish, * the Creator-God, the Sustainer-God, and the Destroyer - God. In retaining youth there comes a conflict between the two Gods, the Creator-God and the Destroyer-God, because the Destroyer-God is destroying and the Creator-God is creating. If the Creator-God in you is stronger, then he will win a victory over the Destroyer-God. Nevertheless, there is nothing that is devoid of beauty in this world. If the soul has received the divine blessing, it will enjoy every aspect of life. Infancy is interesting, childhood has a beauty, youth has its spirit, age has its knowledge and dignity, its wisdom and beauty. There is no note on the piano that has not its particular action, that has not its particular part in the symphony of nature. Whether it is the seventh octave lower or the seventh octave higher, whether it is sharp or flat or natural, whatever key it is, as soon as the harmonious hand touches it, it creates harmony, it makes of this note a symphony. And so we are all as notes before that divine Musician, and when His blessing hand touches, whatever be one's life's condition, whether child or youth or old or young, the beauty will manifest and add to life's symphony.

The mistake is that man wishes to live through the mortal part of his being; that is what brings disappointment. For he

---

*One of the names of Shiva.

knows only that part of his being that is mortal, and he identifies himself with his mortal being. Hardly one among thousands realizes that life lives and death dies. That which lives cannot die; what dies will not live; it is only a phenomenon of life that makes even that which is not living, for the moment, a kind of illusion of life. When we study the dead body—the greatest study we can make—we see that no sooner has life left it than the whole charm of the body has gone. Why is there not that attraction that has always been there? Why is the body void of all beauty and magnetism? Why do those who loved that person retire from his dead body and wish to remove it? What has gone from it, what is dead in it? The part that is subject to death is dead; the life that lived in it is still alive. This body was only covering a life; now that life has left. But the living being is not dead; it is the mortal cover that was covering the life that is dead. Is it not, then, the absence of this knowledge that gives a person fear of death?

What is death, after all? There is a saying of the Prophet that the illuminated souls never fear death. Death is the last thing they fear. And yet one does not fear for anything more than for one's life. One would sacrifice anything in the world—wealth, rank, power or possession—if one could live. If living is an innate desire, then it is most necessary to find the process, the way to get in touch with that real part of ourselves that may be called our being, our self, and thus to become free from what is called mortality. It is the ignorant one who knows only the first floor of his house; by going to the second floor of his house, he thinks that he is dead; he does not know that he has only left the first floor and is going to the second floor. Why does this ignorance exist? Because he never tried to go to the second floor. The first floor is quite enough for him; the second floor does not exist for him, though it is a floor in his own house.

Is immortality to be gained, to be acquired? No, it is to be discovered. One has only to make one's vision keener—in other words, to explore oneself, but that is the last thing one does. People are most pleased to explore the tomb of Tutankhamen in Egypt in order to find mysteries, regardless of the mystery hidden in their own heart. Tell them about any mystery existing outside themselves, and they are delighted to explore it. But when you tell them to see into themselves, they think it is too simple; they think, "I know myself. I am a mortal being. I don't want to die, but death awaits me." They make difficulties, they raise complexities by their own complex intelligence. They do not like the straight way. They like the zigzag way; they enjoy puzzles. Even if there is a door before them, they say, "No, I do not look for it." If a door opens before them, they do not wish to go out by that door; they prefer to be in the puzzle. It is a greater joy not to be able to find the door for a long time. One who is thus enjoying the puzzle is horrified when he sees the way out. The saying of the Prophet is, "Die before death." What does this mean? It does not mean, "Commit suicide." It only means, "Study the condition of death." One need not die. Play it; one should play death and find out what it is. The whole mystical cult is that play—playing death; and that play becomes the means by which to understand the mystery hidden behind life.

Man constitutes in himself spirit and matter. What is matter? Crystallized spirit. What is spirit? The original substance. Spirit may be likened to running water, and matter to ice. But if there is water and ice, the water will run and the ice will stay where it is. It does not mean that ice will not return to its original condition; it will, but its time has not yet come. Therefore the water will proceed first, and the ice will stay where it is; the substance stays where it is, but the life, the spirit, passes away. What is necessary, before this happens, is for a person to make the spirit independent of the mortal covering, even if it be only for a moment. By that the fear of death naturally vanishes, because then one begins to see the condition after death here on earth. This physical cover has imprisoned, so to speak, the soul in it; the soul finds itself in prison and cannot see itself. What it can

see is the cover. Jelal ad-din Rumi explains it most beauti-
fully in a poem he wrote about sleep, because it is in sleep
that the soul naturally becomes independent of this mortal
garb. Rumi says:

> Every night Thou freest our spirits from the body
> And its snare, making them pure as razed tablets.
> Every night spirits are released from this cage,
> And set free, neither lording it nor lorded over.
> At night prisoners are unaware of their prison;
> At night kings are unaware of their majesty.
> Then there is no thought or care for loss or gain;
> No regard to such a one or such a one.

And the continual longing of the soul is for freedom from
this imprisonment. Rumi begins his book, the *Masnavi,* with
this lamentation of the soul longing to free itself. But is it
to free the soul by actual death, by suicide? No! No mystics
have done this; it is not meant to be done. It is by playing
death that one arrives at the knowledge of life and death,
and it is the secret of life that will make the soul free. The
different planes of existence, which are hidden behind the
cover of this physical body, begin to manifest to the person
who plays death. All different methods of concentration and
of meditation that are prescribed by the teacher to the pupil
are all part of that process of playing. In themselves they are
nothing; they are a play. What is important is what one finds
out as an outcome of that play—what one discovers in the
end. Of course, the play begins with self-negation. And a
person who likes to say twenty times in the day, "I," does
not like to say, "I am not, Thou art." But he does not know
that this claim of "I" is the root of all his trouble. It is this
claim that makes him feel hurt by every little insult and
every little disturbance. The amount of pain that this illusion gives him is so great that it is just as well he got rid of
it. But that is the last thing he would do. He would give up
his last penny, but not the thought of "I." He would hold

on to the thought of "I"; it is the dearest thing. That is the whole difficulty and the only hindrance on the spiritual path.

Very often people ask, "How long has one to go on on the spiritual path?" There is no limit to the length of this path, and yet if one is ready, it does not take a long time. It is but a moment and one is there. How true it is, what the wise of past ages said to their followers, "Do not go directly into the temple; first walk fifty times around it!" The meaning was, "First get a little tired, then enter." Then you value it. One values something for which one makes an effort; if it comes without effort, it is nothing to one. If a government should ask a tax for the air one breathes, people would protest against it. Yet they do not know that there is no comparison between the air and the money they possess. The value of the one is incomparably greater than of the other, and yet the most valuable things are attained with the least effort. One simply does not realize their importance. One would rather have something that is attained with a great effort and that may in the end prove to be nothing.

It is very simple to think, "Why should every being have the innate desire to live, if continual life is impossible?" There is no desire in the world that has not its answer. The answer to every desire is somewhere; the fulfillment of every desire must come one day. Therefore, without doubt the desire to live must be fulfilled. And the fulfillment of this desire is in getting above the illusion that is caused by ignorance of the secret of life.

Chapter 4.

THE KNOWLEDGE OF EVERY LIVING SOUL: THE DESIRE FOR KNOWLEDGE

It is the knowledge of the ultimate truth that fulfills the purpose of life.

A curious soul begins by trying to know everything that it sees, everything that it comes in contact with. What it wants to know first is the name of an object, what it is, what it is used for, how to use it, how it is made, how to make the best of it, and how to profit by it to the utmost. This knowledge is what we call learning. The different divisions of learning, called by different names, are the classification of the knowledge that one gains by study of the outside world. But life is so short and the field of this knowledge is so vast that a person may go on and on studying. He may, perhaps, study one branch of knowledge, and he may find that even one entire lifetime is not sufficient to be fully acquainted with that one particular branch of knowledge. And another person may not be satisfied with only touching one branch of knowledge; he wants to touch many branches of knowledge. He may become acquainted, to a certain degree, with different aspects of knowledge. It may perhaps make him, if he reaches somewhere, what might be called an all-around man. Yet that is not the thing that will fulfill the purpose of his life. Farabi, the great Arabian scientist in ancient times, claimed that he knew many sides of knowledge, but when it came to showing his equipment in the knowledge of music, he proved to be lacking in the essential part, which is not the theory of music but the practice of music.

Knowledge can be divided into two aspects: one aspect is the knowledge we call learning, and the other aspect is knowing. Learning comes from reason—"It is so, because of this or that;" that is knowledge. But there is a knowing that cannot be explained by "because." It can only be said that it is so; it cannot be anything else. The knowledge with its "because" attached is contradicted a thousand times over. One scientist, one inventor, one learned person has one argument; another comes and says, "This is not what I think; I have found out the truth about it, which the one who looked before did not perceive rightly." This has always been and will always be so with the outer knowledge. But with that knowing that is the central knowledge there has never been a difference, and there never will be. The saints, sages, seers, mystics, and prophets of all ages, in whatever part of the world they were born, when they have touched this realm of knowing, they have all agreed on this same one thing. It is therefore that they called it Truth. It was not because this was the conception of one person, or the expression of another person, or the doctrine of a certain people, or the teaching of a certain religion. No, it was the knowledge of every knowing soul. And every soul, whether in the past, present, or future, whenever it arrives at the stage when it knows, will realize the same thing. Therefore it is in that knowledge that there is to be found the fulfillment of the purpose of one's coming on the earth.

Now one may ask, "What is that knowledge? How can one attain to it?" The first condition is to separate the outer knowledge from the inner knowing—to separate the real from the unreal. False and true, the two things cannot go together. The knowledge gained from the outer world is the knowledge of the cover of all things, not of the spirit of all things. Therefore, that knowledge cannot be essential knowledge. It is not the knowledge of the spirit of all things but the knowledge of the cover of all things that we study and call learning, and to it we give the greatest importance. One may say, "What is one to do when the call of the intellectual reason for knowledge and learning is such that it threatens one's faith in the possibility of knowledge by the self?" The answer is to go on, in that case, with the intellectual knowledge until one feels satisfied with it or tired of it. For one must not seek after food if one is not hungry. The food that is sought in the absence of hunger will prove to be a poison. Great as it is, the knowledge of self does not manifest if there is not a natural desire for it raging like fire.

One might ask, "Then why should we not try to get to the bottom of all outside things; shall we not by this way reach the same knowledge?" That is not possible. The easiest way and the best possible way is to attain to the knowledge of the self. It is the after-effect of this attainment that will give one keen sight into outside things—into the spirit of outward things. The question is about oneself—the knowledge of self, and what that knowledge is. Do we know ourselves? None of us, for one moment, will think that we do not know ourselves. That is the difficulty. Everyone says, "I know myself better than I know anybody else. What is there to be learned in myself? Is it the anatomy of the body?" Yes, in fact, the first thing is to understand the construction of the body; that is the first lesson.

By the study of the body, one will find that there are five different elements that constitute it. The mystics, for convenience, call them earth, water, fire, air, and ether. But these must not be compared with scientific terms; it is only for the convenience of a mystic. Then one will see the different senses and the organs of the senses: each sense represents one of these elements. And coming to the natural tendencies and needs of life, every action one does has a relation to one of these five elements. The study of this mechanism will make a person understand that something that he always called *himself* is nothing but a mechanism, a mechanism made of five elements, which are borrowed from the outer world. And he will find that his mind, which experiences through all the organs of the senses, still remains aloof, as a spectator who conceives and perceives the outside world through the medium of the mechanism he calls his body. This knowledge will awaken a deep thinker to the fact that he is not his body; although, consciously or unconsciously, there is perhaps one among a million persons who clearly realizes, "My body is my instrument; I am not my body." The one who has come to realize, "My body is my instrument," is the controller of this prison; he is the engineer of this machinery.

Then there comes the next stage of knowing oneself, which is to explore what one calls the mind. By a minute study of the mind, one will find that the different qualities, such as reason, memory, thought, feeling, and the ego—all these five things—constitute mind. One will find that there is a surface to this and there is a depth to it. Its depth is the heart; its surface is mind. Each quality of mind represents one of these five elements. This again takes us to the thought that even the mind, which is above the physical body, is a mechanism. And the more one is acquainted with the mechanism, the more one is able to manage it to its best advantage; and it is the ignorance of the secret of this mechanism that keeps man unaware of his own domain. This knowledge makes one think, "I am neither my body nor am I my mind; I am the engineer who has these two possessions, these two machineries, to work with to the best advantage in life." Then one begins to ask, "What am I?" For to a certain degree even the mind is a mechanism that is borrowed from the outer sphere, as the body is a mechanism that has been borrowed from the physical plane—that has been gathered together and constructed. Therefore, neither mind nor body is the self. One thinks "It is myself" only because one cannot see oneself. And so one says of everything one sees, "This is myself." The self becomes acquainted with everything but itself. So the mind, which the self has used, has become a kind of cover upon the light that fulfills the purpose of life.

When this is intellectually realized, although it does not fulfill the purpose, it begins one's journey in the search of truth. This must be realized by the process of meditation, the process by which the self can separate itself from the body and afterwards from the mind. For the self, deluded all through life, is not ready to understand and is not prepared to understand truth. It rejects truth; it fights truth. It is like the story told in my *Divan*, in which a lion saw a lion cub wandering through the wilderness with the sheep. The lion was very surprised, and instead of running after the sheep, he ran after this lion cub, and the little lion was trembling and very frightened. The father lion said, "Come, my son, with me; you are a lion." "No," said the cub. "I tremble, I tremble, I am afraid of you. You are different from my playmates. I want to run with them, play with them; I want to be with them." "Come, my son, with me," said the lion, "you are a little lion." "No," said the cub, "no, I am not a lion. You are a lion; I am afraid of you." The lion said, "I will not let you go; you must come with me." The lion took him to the shore of the lake and said, "Now look in it and see with your own eyes if you are a lion or if you are a sheep." This explains what initiation means, and what the initiator teaches to his disciple as meditation. Once the image is reflected in the lake of the heart, self-knowledge comes by itself.

Chapter 5.

TO DENY SELF AND AFFIRM GOD: THE DESIRE FOR POWER

Seek ye first the Kingdom of God, and all things shall be added unto you.— Luke 12:31

It is the desire for all one wishes to achieve that gives one the desire for power. One desires power in order to hold something, to make something, to attain something, to work out something, to attract something, to use something, to rule something, to assimilate something. If it is a natural desire, there is an answer to this. For there cannot be a desire to which there is no answer; the answer to the desire is in knowing that desire fully. Whatever power is gained by outside efforts in life, however great it may seem for the moment, it proves fatal when it comes to be examined. Even such great powers as the nations that existed just before the war*took no time to fall to pieces. There was an army, there was a navy, there was property, there was a state. An empire

*Before the First World War.

24

such as the empire of Russia—how long it took to build it! But it did not take one moment for it to break up. If the outer power, in spite of its great appearance for the moment, proves fatal in the end, then there must be some power hidden somewhere that may be called worthwhile; and that power is hidden in man.

A person in the intoxication of whatever outer power he possesses overlooks the cultivation or the development of inner power, and, depending upon the power that does not belong to him, one day becomes the victim of the very power that he holds, because when the outer power becomes greater and the inner smaller, the greater power eats up the inner power. So it is that the heroes, the kings, the emperors, the persons with great power of arms, wealth, or outer influence, have become victims of the very power upon which they always depended. So one thinks, "If the outer power is not to be depended upon, then where is that power to be found upon which one can depend?" That power is to be found in oneself. What power is it? In the terms of the Sufis, that power is called *iman,* conviction. And how is that power built? That power is built by what the Sufis call *yaqin,* which means belief. It is belief that culminates in conviction. The one who has no inclination to believe will never arrive at a conviction.

But now there is a question. Is even a power developed in one's personality not a limited power? True, it is a limited power. But by following that teaching that Christ has given in the words, "Seek ye first the kingdom of God and all things shall be added unto you," that power that is unlimited is gained. If not, there is no meaning in calling God "Almighty." The benefit of the word "almighty" is in its realization. This teaches us in the first place that all might is one might. Although outwardly we see different powers, one greater than another, either in harmony or in conflict— limited powers working for or against one another—yet by inward realization one finds that there is but one power. In support of this the Qur'an says that nothing is powerful except it shows the same one power, the power of the All-powerful. In other words, in the limited aspect, which we see, and in its absolute being, there is only one Power. And, therefore, there is no might to stand against that power we call Almighty Power, there is no power to work against it; all aspects of strength and power are from it, and in it, and will be assimilated by it in the end.

As long as man is striving for power, as everyone is striving in some way or other, without the knowledge of that all-sufficient power there will always be a disappointment. For he will always find limitation. His ideal will always go forward and he will find himself short of power. It is only by getting in touch with the Almighty Power that he will begin to realize the All-powerful and the phenomena of the Almighty.

Now the question is, "How can one get in touch with that Almighty Power?" As long as one's little personality stands before one, as long as one cannot get rid of it, as long as one's own person and all that is connected with it interest one, one will always find limitations. That Power is touched only by one way, and that is the way of self-effacement, which in the Bible is called self-denial. People interpret it otherwise. Self-denial, they say, means to deny oneself all the happiness and pleasures of this earth. If it were to deny the happiness and pleasures of this earth, then why was this earth made? Only to deny? If it was made to deny, it was very cruel. For the continual seeking of man is for happiness. Self-denying is to deny this little personality that creeps into everything, to efface this false ego, which prompts one to feel one's little power in this thing or that thing; to deny the idea of one's own being, the being that one knows to be oneself, and to affirm God in that place; to deny self and affirm God. That is the perfect humility. When a person shows politeness by saying, "I am only a humble little creature," perhaps he is hiding in his words. It is his vanity, and therefore that humility is of no use. When one completely denies oneself, there are no words to speak. What can one

TO DENY SELF AND AFFIRM GOD 27

say? Praise and blame become the same to one; there is nothing to be said. And how is this to be attained? It is to be attained not only by prayer or by worship or by believing in God; it is to be attained by forgetting oneself in God. The belief in God is the first step. By the belief in God is attained the losing of oneself in God. If one is able to do this, one has attained a power that is beyond human comprehension. The process of attaining this is called *fana* by the Sufis. Fana is not necessarily a destruction in God. Fana results in what may be called a resurrection in God, which is symbolized by the picture of Christ. The Christ on the cross is a narrative of fana; it means, "I am not." And the idea of resurrection explains the next stage, which is *baqa*, and which means, "Thou art," and this means rising towards All-might. The divine spirit is to be recognized in that rising towards All-might. Fana is not attained by torturing oneself, by tormenting oneself, or by giving oneself a great many troubles, as many ascetics do. For even after torturing themselves, they will not come to that realization if they were not meant to. That realization is attained by denying one's self, the false self that covers one's real self, in which the essence of divine Being is to be found.

Chapter 6.

THE DESIRE FOR HAPPINESS

*The very fact that man is continually craving for happi-
ness shows that the real element, which may be called
man's real being, is not what has formed his body and
what has composed his mind, but what he is in himself.*

Happiness, which is sought after by every soul, has its secret
in the knowledge of the self. Man seeks happiness, not
because happiness is his sustenance, but because happiness
is his own being. Therefore, in seeking happiness, man is
seeking for himself. What gives man the inclination to seek
for happiness is the feeling of having lost something he had
always owned, which belonged to him, which was his own
self. The absence of happiness, which a soul has experienced
from the day it came on earth and which has increased more
and more every day, makes man forget that his own being
is happiness. He thinks that happiness is something that is
acquired. As man thinks happiness is something that is acquired, he continually strives in every direction to attain it.
In the end, after all his striving, he finds that the real happi-

ness does not lie in what he calls pleasures. Pleasures may be a shadow of happiness; there is an illusion of happiness, because all the illusion that stands beside reality is more interesting for the average man than reality itself.

A happiness that is momentary, a happiness that depends upon something outside of oneself, is called pleasure. Very often we confuse, in our everyday language, the distinction between pleasure and happiness. A pastime, an amusement, merriment, gaiety that take one's thoughts away from the responsibilities and worries and limitations of life and give one a moment's consolation—one begins by thinking that these are the ways of happiness. But as one cannot hold them, and as one often finds that, seeking for what may be called a pleasure, the loss is greater than the gain, then one begins to look for something that will really be the means of happiness. It is this, very often that awakens a soul to look for the mystery of religion, for the sense in philosophy, for the secret of mysticism, in case he can find some happiness there. But even all these things only help one to find happiness; they are not happiness themselves. It is the soul that is happiness itself, not all outer things that man seeks after and that he thinks will give him happiness. The very fact that man is continually craving for happiness shows that the real element, which may be called man's real being, is not what has formed his body and what has composed his mind, but what he is in himself.

The mind and body are vehicles. Through the mind and body man experiences life more fully, more clearly; but they are not happiness in themselves, nor does what is experienced through them give real happiness. What we experience through them is just pleasure, an illusion of happiness for a time. It is not only that the pleasures cost more than they are worth, but very often in the path of pleasure, when a person is seeking after happiness, as he goes further, he creates more and more unhappiness for himself. This happens very often. Every way he turns, everything he does, every plan he carries out thinking that this will give him happiness only produces a greater trouble, because he is seeking after happiness in a wrong direction.

A person might ask, "Is, then, the secret of happiness in the way of the ascetics, in tormenting and torturing oneself as they have done for ages?" Even that does not give happiness; it is only a distraction from the worldly pleasures that produce illusion. The ascetic shuts himself up in order to have an opportunity to take another direction. But very often it so happens that the one who lives an ascetic life is himself unaware of what he is doing and what it is intended for. And therefore even if he lives his whole life as an ascetic, he cannot derive a full benefit from it. His loss is then greater than his gain. For even asceticism is not a happiness; it is only a means of self-discipline; it is a drill in order to fight against temptations that draw one continually in life and hinder one's path to happiness. Not understanding this, a person may go on living an ascetic life, but can never be benefited by it, like a soldier who has drilled all his life and never fought. Many have understood self-denial as the way to happiness, and they interpret self-denial in the form of asceticism—to deny oneself all pleasures that are momentary. There is another point from which to look at it: the creation is not intended to be renounced. We read in the Qur'an that God has made all that is in the heavens and on the earth subservient to man. For this reason, all that is beautiful and pleasing, all that gives joy and pleasure, is not to be renounced. The secret of all this is that what is made for man, man may hold, but he must not be held by it.

When man renounces the path of happiness, real happiness, in order to pursue pleasures, it is then that he does wrong. If in the pursuit of the happiness that is the ultimate happiness he goes on through life, then for him to be an ascetic and deny himself all pleasures is not necessary. There is a story told of Solomon that he had a vision in which God revealed Himself to him and said "Ask what I shall give thee." Solomon said, " Give me an understanding heart, wisdom and knowledge." And God said to him, "Because thou hast asked this thing and has not asked long life for thyself, neither hast thou asked riches for thyself, but hast asked for thyself understanding, behold, I have done according to thy word; I have given thee a wise and an understanding heart. And I have also given thee that which thou hast not asked, both riches and honor, and I will lengthen thy days." This shows that the true way is not the renouncing of things, but making the best use of them, making the right use of them; it is not going away from life, but being among the crowd, being in the midst of life and yet not being attached to it. One might say that it would be a cruel thing to be detached from anybody who wants our love and kindness and sympathy. You can attach yourself to the whole world if you will not be of the world. If one keeps one's thoughts centered upon the idea of the real happiness that is attained by the realization of the self, and if one does not allow anything to hinder that, then in the end one arrives at that happiness that is the purpose of the coming on earth of every soul.

Chapter 7.

THE DESIRE FOR PEACE

*There is no pleasure in the world, however great, and
no experience, however interesting, that gives one the
satisfaction that peace alone can give.*

The secret behind the whole manifestation is vibration, vibration which may be termed movement. It is the differences of vibration that, when divided by lines, form planes of existence, each plane being different in the rhythm of these vibrations. When we take life as a whole we can draw one line, the beginning and the end, or spirit and matter, or God and man. And we shall find that the rhythm that begins the line is fine and without disturbance, and the rhythm that is felt at the end of the line is gross and disturbing. These two rhythms may be named the life of peace and the life of sensation.

These are two opposite things. The life of sensation gives a momentary joy; the life that is in fact the first aspect of life gives peace and culminates in the everlasting peace. Joy, however great, rises and falls; it must have its reaction. Besides, it depends upon sensation; and what does sensation depend upon? Sensation depends upon the outer life; there must be something besides you to cause the sensation. But peace is independently felt within oneself; it is not dependent upon the outer sensation. It is something that belongs to one, something that is one's own self. If one were to ask someone who lives continually in a kind of excitement of worldly pleasures, whom Providence has granted all pleasures imaginable, if that person were asked, "What do you wish besides all this that you experience?" he will say, "To be left alone." When madness comes, when he is out of balance, he will crave for sensation, but when that passion has gone, what he is longing for in reality is peace. Therefore there is no pleasure in the world, however great, and no experience, however interesting, that can give one the satisfaction that peace alone can give. A sovereign may be happy sitting on the throne with his crown, with many attendants before him, but he is only satisfied when he is alone by himself. All else seems to him nothing; it has no value; the most precious thing for him is that moment when he is by himself.

I have seen the Nizam,* a great ruler, in all his grandeur, enjoying the royal splendor around him, and then again I saw the same sovereign sitting alone on a little carpet, and it was at that time that he was himself. It is the same with everyone. Delicious dishes, sweet fragrance, music, all the pleasures of line and color, and beauty in all its aspects, all of which seem to answer one's life's demands, fail in the end when compared with that satisfaction that a soul experiences in itself, which it feels to be its own property, its own belonging; something that one need not seek outside oneself, that one can find within oneself, and something that is incomparably greater and more valuable than anything else in the world; something that cannot be bought or sold, something that cannot be robbed by anyone, and something

*H. E. H. Mahbub Ali Khan, Sixth Nizam of Hyderabad, died 1911.

that is more sacred and holy than religion or prayer. For the purpose of all prayer and devotion is to attain to this peace.

A man good and kind, a person most learned and qualified, strong and powerful, with all these attributes, cannot be spiritual if his soul has not attained that rhythm that is a natural rhythm of its being—a rhythm in which alone exists life's satisfaction. Peace is not knowledge, peace is not power, peace is not happiness, but peace is all these; and, besides, peace is productive of happiness, peace inspires one with knowledge of the seen and unseen, and in peace is to be found the divine Presence. It is not the excited one who conquers in this continual battle of life; it is the peaceful one who tolerates all, who forgives all, who understands all, who assimilates all things. The one who lacks peace, with all his possessions—whether property of this earth or quality of mind—is still poor. He has not got that wealth that may be called divine, and without which man's life is useless. For true life, a life that will not be robbed by death, is in peace. The secret of mysticism, the mystery of philosophy, all is to be attained after the attainment of peace. You cannot refuse to recognize the divine in a person who is a person of peace. It is not the talkative, it is not the argumentative one, who proves to be wise. He may have intellect and worldly wisdom, and yet may not have pure intelligence, which is real wisdom. True wisdom is to be found in the peaceful, for peacefulness is the sign of wisdom. It is the peaceful one who is observant: it is peace that gives him the power to observe keenly. It is the peaceful one, therefore, who can conceive, for peace helps him to conceive. It is the peaceful who can contemplate; one who has no peace cannot contemplate properly. Therefore all things pertaining to spiritual progress in life depend upon peace.

And now the question is, what makes one lack peace? The answer is, love of sensation. A person who is always seeking to experience life in movement, in activity, in whatever form, wants more and more of that experience. In the end he becomes dependent upon the life that is outside, and so he loses in the end his peace—the peace that is his real self. When a person says about someone, "That person has lost his soul" the soul is not lost; the soul has lost its peace. Absorption in the outer life, every moment of the day and night, thinking and worrying and working and fighting, struggling along, in the end rob one of one's soul. Even if one gains as the price of that fighting something that is outside oneself, someone who is a greater fighter still will snatch it from his grasp one day.

One might ask if it is not our necessity in life that keeps us absorbed in the outer life and does not give us a moment to experience peace. In answer to this I must say: suppose the outer life has taken ten hours of the day, you still have two hours; if sleep has taken ten hours of the day, you still have two hours to spare. To attain peace, what one has to do is to seek that rhythm that is in the depth of our being. It is just like the sea: the surface of the sea is ever-moving; the depth of the sea is still. And so it is with our life. If our life is thrown into the sea of activity, it is on the surface; we still live in the profound depths, in that peace. But the thing is to become conscious of that peace that can be found within ourselves. It is this that can bring us the answer to all our problems. If not, when we want to solve one problem, there is another difficult problem coming. There is no end to our problems; there is no end to the difficulties of the outer life. And if we get excited over them, we shall never be able to solve them. Some think, "We might wait; perhaps the conditions will become better; we shall see then what to do." But when will the conditions become better? They will become still worse! Whether the conditions become better or worse, the first thing is to seek the kingdom of God within ourselves, in which there is peace; as soon as we have found that, we have found our support, we have found our self. And in spite of all the activity and movement on the surface, we shall be able to keep that peace undisturbed if only we hold it fast by becoming conscious of it.

Chapter 8.

THE FREEDOM OF THE SOUL (I)

Freedom is the soul's true nature. It is a captive in mind and in body. The whole tragedy of the soul is its captivity.

Freedom is such that it is desired by every creature. From this we see that it is the soul's tendency and the spirit's longing to become free. Animals and birds, however carefully educated and tended by us, still have the instinct to avoid being confined.

Where does the desire for freedom begin? Its beginning is explained in a very beautiful way in some of the ancient stories. The stories from the Hebrew and Arabic scriptures tell us that when God made Adam He commanded the spirit to enter the body of Adam, which He had made out of clay and water. When the spirit was commanded to enter, it refused, saying, "No, I will never become a captive in this dark prison, I who have always been free, dwelling anywhere without bondage, without barrier. I will never become captive in this place." Then God said to the angels,

36

"Sing." And when they sang, the spirit fell into ecstasy; it became intoxicated by the beauty of the singing. While in this state of intoxication it did not know whither it was going, and thus it was that it entered the required place. So when Adam opened his eyes, the spirit was there. Adam was alive.

When we inquire into the tragedy of life, the very first of all causes is the separation from freedom. This tragedy can be seen in all kinds of people. From rich to poor, from the most illiterate to the most educated, every one has this grudge. Maybe one confesses it while another does not, but the grudge is in everybody's mind just the same; that he has entered this objective world. For this entry seems to be the cause of all the tragedy of life, the tragedy that man's spirit cannot be satisfied in life, cannot have lasting happiness, as long as he stays in it.

But if you ask someone you meet what the cause of his life's tragedy is, he may say, "Oh, that I long to have more money; I am very poor, and without resources I am so unhappy." Another person may say, "Oh, I have everything I want, but my relatives are quarrelsome and very unkind to me." Another says, "I have everything I want but good health." A fourth says, "I have everthing, but I long to have certain peace." Another, "I long to accomplish this art; that big purpose in life; not having done so makes me unhappy."

And if you were to supply to each his life's need, giving money to the poor man, harmony to the man without harmony, position to the man who has not got it, a beautiful palace to the one who longs for that, health to him who does not have it, then see how long he would remain happy! It would be only for that moment when his desire was fulfilled, and then he would again feel the hunger for he knows not what. He asks his mind, "What more do I want?" and his mind says, "You feel so unhappy." And as soon as he asks, "For what?" his mind answers that he cannot have that which he seeks.

It is in this way that all through his life a man runs after things which are not the real desire of his soul. Sometimes he thinks it is his bodily appetites and passions which demand satisfaction, sometimes that it is his intellectual powers; but even if they were satisfied he would still find himself unhappy. "Perhaps," he thinks, "it is wealth, position, or honors that are lacking." Or he thinks, "It is not that I do not have the things I need, but I have not enough of them. If he has a motorcar, he is unhappy because he has no chauffeur.

His mind, his reason, always puts forward some other cause for his unhappiness rather than the real one, in order that he may be kept in illusion all his life, in order that all his life he should run after things which are not the real aim of his soul. Throughout his whole life he seeks after things, trying first this, then that. One day he buys this, another that, and after getting these things he still thinks, "Oh, there is still something else, that is why I am unhappy," and as long as he does not have it, he considers that the cause. If he has ten things he wants twenty; if he acquires twenty he seeks thirty; if he has thirty he desires fifty; and so on. Indeed if he had thousands and billions, he would want a kingdom; after that a whole universe. And if the whole universe were given to him, his heart would not be satisfied, because the demand of his soul still has not been understood. He goes through life mourning and sorrowing for things he cannot get, not understanding in what lie true gain and true loss.

Therefore, when a seer or one who has realized life looks at this world, he sees that however old a person may be— aged, young, middle-aged—he is still like a child. Children become very unhappy because they do not have, or cannot get a toy, a toy to which grown-ups would not attach any importance. To the seer, the desires of ordinary grown-up people are also like toys. The things that matter to the world do not matter to him. This is the sign that one has realized the aim of his soul.

For the aim of the soul is freedom. Freedom is the soul's

true nature. It is a captive in mind and in body. The whole tragedy of the soul is its captivity. All names such as *nirvana* or *mukti,* salvation or liberation are those of the one aim or ideal of the soul throughout our whole life. Yet hardly anyone knows what it is he aims at. All that he does know is that there is such a longing, and that hope is constantly there.

Everyone wakes in the morning as if he were expecting something. Everyone goes to bed with the thought, "Perhaps tommorrow or the day after tomorrow I shall obtain my heart's desire." With some the desire is for a position or a friend; with others it is a hope. Everyone is looking out as if waiting for that something to come.

There is a familiar saying, "Wait till my ship comes in." Every soul is waiting for his ship to come, not knowing what that ship will bring or what sort of ship it is. Still, every soul is looking the "my ship," every soul is unconsciously waiting for the coming of "my ship." One person thinks it is the prospering of trade, another of business; another thinks it is the coming of power or position; but everyone believes the ship will come.

The ship is different according to whether it is pictured by the mind or the body or the soul. The ship of the soul is its freedom. Indeed, freedom is the real object in all aspects of life: if the desire is for wealth, it is nothing but a desire for freedom from poverty; if the desire is for power, it is nothing but a desire for freedom to act as one wishes. The ideal of every soul is freedom, freedom to work, freedom to act, freedom to think, freedom in every direction.

Not knowing that this is the heart's real desire, man has always, from the first day of his creation, neglected the true freedom because of his pursuit of freedom in the external life. That has been his mistake. In spite of the little freedom he has thus gained he finds himself a captive still; he has still failed to gain the complete joy and peace that his soul longs for.

Freedom for the body would be the freedom of walking

in gardens or moving about wherever it wished. But that would not be freedom for the mind: the mind would still be captive. Suppose the mind had freedom, freedom of thought, of understanding, of imagination, of action. Even then the soul would still be captive. But if the soul is free, the mind is free and the body is also free.

How do we attain to this freedom? In the Sanskrit language there is a very expressive word for freedom, *taran,* which means "liberation," "swimming," or "floating." It is such a beautiful idea that swimming and liberation are alike in their nature.

How true it is, as the eastern poets have always said, "Life is a *bhava sagara,* an ocean into which all things are drawn, fall, and are absorbed." It sweeps away all the plants and trees, animals and birds, and all that lies in the path of the flood. All are borne away into the ocean, for such is its force and power. Similarly, this life sweeps away all the trees and plants, animals and men. Everything that we see is here only for the moment, and then it is swept away. There is always a certain period after which the things that seemed so enduring all disappear. If they came back, our ancestors would not recognize the country, the houses, the trees, the manners; everything would be different. All that was familiar to them has been swept away. That is the story of this life. That is why it is called *maya,* the illusion created before us like a dream in the night. In the morning, it has all gone away. All the happiness, unhappiness, pleasures, horrors—whatever we experience in the night, in the morning we perceive it to have been a dream.

When we come to think of it, the whole of creation is not in the end what we thought it was: manners, customs, faces, everything is changed. That is the condition of life. It is just like the sea: the tide comes, and it sweeps all before it, flowers, fruit, and all. Therefore life is pictured by the thinkers of the East as an ocean into which everything is swept.

The miracle of Christ walking on the water is understood

by mystics as teaching a mystery. Walking on water expresses the idea which in Sanskrit is called taran, to float or swim. To swim one must have one's head above water. We avoid the water which sweeps us away in order to preserve that existence which our soul longs to save. Our body is alive as our mind and our soul are alive, and it does not want to be non-existent: it desires to continue to exist. However unhappy or feeble a man may be, his life is too dear to him to be sacrificed. Suicide is only possible under great emotional stress. All work, all struggles are in order to live. All fights, all disagreements, all money-seeking, all comfort-seeking are in order to live. All through life it is one struggle to live, yet the true life is not realized.

Christ, from first to last, teaches the reality of eternal life. His only lesson was life. It is the desire of the soul to live, and that life is the real life. Man keeps imagining that his life is for eating delicious dishes, for making merry, or for being comfortable for the time being. But when the body is gone, how will he live? What will become of his comforts? When the mind is not there, how will he satisfy the mind? To live in the body or the mind is to live in vehicles upon which one becomes dependent but which must pass and be no more.

Therefore the lesson that we must learn is how to swim, how to float, how to prevent ourselves from sinking in the flood of death or mortality. How shall we avoid that? The answer is found when we understand that man is travelling in a boat and the boat is heavily laden. The storm comes on, and the one who is rowing says to the man, "The storm is severe, your luggage is very heavy; the best thing will be for you to save your life by throwing one of your bundles into the water." The man says, "Oh, that bundle contains things I have collected all my life, and I cannot throw it out." "Well," says the boatman, "if you cannot throw it out you will drown."

When the passenger has thrown out one bundle, perhaps

the storm becomes greater, and maybe then the last bundle has to be thrown away as well. And he says, "Oh, I can never part with this one! It contains things I have collected all through my life; they are souvenirs, and you want me to throw them away! Things from my grandfather and my great-grandfather—do you really want me to throw them away?" The other says, "If not, you will go also. If you want to save your life, throw that last bundle away too!"

That is what death does with mankind. It says, "You are so interested in your vehicle, which you call your body," and so first of all he sends disease. That is the first step. The person who thinks so much of his body is always ill. He is very conscientious about his body, saying, "This is the one thing I must keep well-preserved." He goes on thinking of it too much, and so he feels ill. And in the end he has to throw both bundles away, body and mind.

Others will say that they do not care for their body but only for their mind. They take care of their own imaginations, their own standards of thinking, "What you say is wrong; what I say is right." They are occupied with thoughts, with pursuits, with arguments, saying, "Am I right? Are you? Is she?" And they are all the time in doubt and constant worry, all the time occupied in a struggle about something which is really nothing. To the seer it matters not at all.

And then the tide—death—comes, and they are swept away: the mind goes, the body goes, and the soul returns to its own source. This is a picture of mortality, when mind departs from body with the impression of death.

There is a story which explains this subject very well. It is of a king who had a parrot which he loved so much that he kept it in a golden cage and always attended to it himself. The king and queen both paid such great attention to the parrot that everyone in the palace was jealous of it.

One day the king was about to go into the forest that the parrot came from, and he said to it, "My pet, I have loved you and kept you with all the care and attention and fondness that I could, and I should like very much to take any message you wish to your brothers in the forest." The parrot said, "How kind of you to have offered to do this for me. Convey to my brothers in the jungle that the king and queen have done their very best to make me happy—a golden cage, all kinds of fruits, and nice things of all sorts—and they love me so much. But in spite of all the attention they give me I long for the forest, and the desire to dwell among you, free as I used to be, always possesses my mind. But I see no way out of it, so pray send me your goodwill and your love. One only lives in hope. Perhaps someday my wish will be granted."

The king went into the forest and approached the tree from which the parrot had been taken. He said to the brothers of the parrot, "O parrots, there is one whom I have taken from among you to my palace; and I am very fond of him, and he receives all the attention I can give. This is your brother's message." They listened to the message very attentively, and one after the other dropped to the ground and seemed dead.

The king was depressed beyond measure. Spellbound, he could not understand what he had said that should have affected the feelings of those parrots so much. The loving parrots could not bear his message. And he thought, "What a sin I have committed, to have destroyed so many lives."

He returned to his palace and went to his parrot and said, "How foolish, O Parrot, to give me such a message that as soon as your brothers heard it, one after another they dropped down and all lay dead before me."

The parrot listened to this, and looked up gently to the sky, and then fell down too. The king was even more sad. "How foolish I was! First I gave his message to them and killed them, and now I give their message to him and kill him also." It was all most bewildering to the king. What was the meaning of it all?

He commanded his servants to put his dead parrot on a gold tray, and bury him with all ceremony. The servants took him out of the cage with great respect, and loosed the chains from his feet; and then, as they were laying him out, the parrot suddenly flew away and sat upon the roof.

The king said, "O Parrot, you betrayed me." The parrot said, "O King, this was the aim of my soul, and it is the aim of all souls. My brothers in the jungle were not dead. I had asked them to show me the way to freedom, and they showed me. I did as they told me, and now I am free."

There is a sura in the Qur'an which says: *Mutu kubla anta mutu,* which means, "Die before death." A poet says, "Only he attains to the peace of the Lord who loses himself." God said to Moses, "No man shall see Me and live." To see God we must be non-existent.

What does all this mean? It means that when we see our being with open eyes, we see that there are two aspects to our being: the false and the true. The false life is that of this body and mind, which only exist as long as the life is within. In the absence of that life the body cannot go on. We mistake the true life for the false and the false for the true.

Dying is this: when there is a fruit or something sweet and good to taste, the child comes to its mother and says, "Will you give it to me?" Although it would have given pleasure to the mother to eat it, she gives it to the child. The eating of it by the child is enjoyed by the mother. That is death. She enjoys her life in the joy of another. Those who rejoice in the joy of another though at their own expense have taken the first step towards true life. If we are pleased by giving another a good coat which we would have liked to wear ourselves, if we enjoy that, we are on the first step. If we enjoy a beautiful thing so much that we would like to have it, and then give that joy to another, enjoying it through his experience, we are dead; that is our death, yet we live more than he. Our life is much vaster, deeper, greater.

Seemingly it is a renunciation, an annihilation, but in truth it is a mastery. The real meaning of crucifixion is to crucify this false self and so resurrect the true self. As long as the false self is not crucified, the true self is still not realized. Sufis call it *fana,* annihilation. All the attempts made by true sages and seekers after real truth are for the one aim of attaining to everlasting life.

Chapter 9.

THE FREEDOM OF THE SOUL (II)

When one's soul is free then there is nothing in this world that binds one; everywhere one will breathe freedom, in heaven and on earth.

Man seeks freedom and pursues captivity. There is not one single person whom the word "freedom" does not touch, and there is not one person who does not long for freedom.

At the same time, if we look closely at human life we see that man pursues captivity in some form or other, whether he seeks freedom or not. The soul of man is a dweller in heaven: it is able to see more than the eyes can see; it is able to hear more than the ears can hear. The soul is able to expand further than man can journey; the soul is able to dive deeper than any depths that man can ever touch; the soul is able to reach higher than man can reach by any means. Its life is freedom. It knows nothing but joy and sees nothing but beauty. Its own nature is peace, and its being is life itself. It is not intelligent; it is intelligence itself. It is spirit; its nature is not human but divine. It is for this reason that the soul feels a limitation continually, all through life, as a fish will feel when it is out of water and a bird when its wings are clipped.

If someone asked, "What is the reason of pain?" the answer would be that if we were to summarize in one word the reason of all the pain we see in the world, it is limitation. And where does this limitation come from? From a heavenly being turning into an earthly being. There is nothing to be surprised at when we see that hardly anyone seems to be perfectly happy in life. A rich man has his tale to tell, a poor man has his story; a wise man has his complaint to make, a foolish man has his own legend. And so everyone has something to say. And what they all have to say is the same thing and that is: limitation.

What one pursues, what one seeks after, is a feeling of freedom. And yet nearly everyone pursues freedom wrongly. The nature of life is such that whenever a person thinks, "That will make me free," that in itself makes him more captive, though he cannot realize this until he gets it. As long as he does not have it he believes it will make him free. And so life goes on. Man goes on in the pursuit of freedom, and what he gets is captivity. With all the talk about freedom today, life is more a life of captivity than ever before. Man lives in captivity because he does not think enough about the real meaning of freedom. The more he thinks, the more he will find that as he pursues the path of freedom every step brings him closer to captivity.

Today in this world of science, where materialism prevails, there are fewer every day who believe in such a thing as the soul. They say, "The only thing we know about is the body; if there is a soul, we have never seen it." It is true that nothing comes out of nothing, but their idea is that as the human being is the flower of this tree of manifestation, intelligence must have developed gradually through the mineral, vegetable, and animal kingdoms until it manifested more fully in man. But how can matter develop into intelligence? It is intelligence which is the source of all, but it is the captivity of intelligence in matter which we see. That is why it seems to us that manifestation begins from matter, and as it manifests in man we think man is a development of matter. In reality man identifies himself wrongly with the material part of his being, for the body is only a cover over the real man. The real man is soul itself. And when one says, "I do not see the soul, I see my body," my answer is that the eyes can never see themselves, though they can see all other things; and as the soul is intelligence, it can see all other things but it cannot see itself.

The very fact that it cannot see itself makes it the real self. Besides, all things that we can point out, which are intelligible to ourselves, we call "mine;" and so we call our body "my" body. Naturally the body is not the self, but as man does not know himself he thinks it is. If an actor were to play on the stage with a mask on, those who saw him would recognize the mask, but they would not know what was behind it. So it is with the soul. The manifestation of the soul is only seen through the body; therefore one identifies oneself with the body, and this keeps one ignorant of the soul.

If the soul is intelligence, where does it come from, what is it in essence? All the scriptures of the past, as well as most philosophers, agree that the source and goal of all things is the Intelligent One. But if it is the intelligence itself, why call it the "Intelligent One?" Because it is a being; it is not a thing nor is it a condition. It is first a being, and then it is all conditions and all things. It is a great mistake when a man considers himself as a being, a person, recognizing his own personality, and when it comes to the source and goal of all things he calls it a force, an intelligence. People want so much to get away from the idea of a person behind all that they prefer to say "gods" instead of "God." Instead of calling Him the divine Being, they say "forces;" they would like to turn into plurality the source and goal which remains one and the same through the whole process and all stages of evolution. The oneness of the Spirit is so great that even in this world of variety there is one Spirit and one Being.

In all ages, prophets and masters, thinkers and philosophers have taught that the ultimate aim of philosophy and mysticism is to attain to the freedom of the soul. This truth is disclosed in many different ceremonies, sacred legends, and philosophies. Whatever be man's longing in life, whatever his life's pursuit, his object of attainment, behind it all there is only one and that is the craving of the soul to become free from all bondage. Man does not want to think about that which will make him free when he is absorbed in getting things in life; he does not give a thought to freedom but only to what he pursues for that moment. Perhaps if he gave a thought to the real condition of life he would become different: his attitude would change, his outlook would become wider, and he would not attach so much importance to the things he usually thinks important.

If one asks what kind of captivity it is, the answer is that for a spider the thin threads of the web are a captivity, and for an elephant iron chains are a captivity. The stronger a person is, the greater the captivity; the greater power he has, the greater are his difficulties; the stronger the soul is, the heavier the load it has to carry. Therefore in captivity we are all equal. When a person sees only the surface, it appears as if one has an easy life and another has to toil all day; as if one has a gay life and another is miserable. But that is the outside. When we look deeply into life, we see that, whether a person looks cheerful or sad, in some way or another some captivity is always hidden there. We do not know. In order to understand others' life situation it is not enough to cast a glance at people from the outside. We see only the prisoners; if we saw the prisons we would be shocked.

I have met numberless people who do not know what they want to do next week; they think only of today. Life is becoming uncertain and its burden greater. It is said that we are progressing. But towards what? Freedom? No, towards captivity. A greater and greater load of duty and responsibility is put on our shoulders. Perhaps it is worse in the West, perhaps it is worse in the East; but the cause of it all is the lack of understanding of freedom. One must not look at the earth to see the sun or the moon; one must look in another direction. How to die before death is something that man today does not know and he does not care to know. The central theme of life today is self-assertion. When a person speaks about himself he wants to make himself ten times more important than he is. He cannot help it; if he does not do so others will not understand. Once I even heard one man say to another, "Your modesty is your greatest misfortune."

Every man has to be self-asserting, continually guarding his interests in order to live. There are many who toil from morning till evening, guarding their self-interest and thinking about nothing else. And what is it all for? In order to exist. But even germs and grubs exist and enjoy life much more! Birds fly in the air and are quite happy, but man is loading his heart with a thousand troubles, making his responsibilities greater and greater. And in the end he gains nothing: his health is spoiled, his spirit wrecked. He does not know anymore where he is nor where his spirit is. And if he has nothing here, he has nothing in the hereafter. Many die without ever having given a thought to the deeper side of life. Not that they did not care for it but they could not find time for it; they had too much to do in life.

One might ask, "Why is this condition so tragic? Why can it not be improved?" The answer is that it is natural. What is man? Man is a process; manifestation is a process through which the spirit goes from one condition to another condition, from one pole to another pole. And through this whole process the attempt of the spirit is to find itself. In this process the spirit first loses its freedom; freedom is lost in order to arrive at freedom. That is the tragedy. Yet in the end there is happiness, for the whole of creation was intended for the fulfillment of this object.

Tragedy appeals to every thinking soul, to every feeling heart. Why? Because tragedy is going on continually. Man would like to get away from tragedy, but it appeals to him because the soul is always in that condition; it is longing for freedom, though it does not know what it is.

The highest perception of freedom comes when a person has freed himself from the false ego, when he is no longer what he was. All the different kinds of freedom will give a momentary sensation of being free, but true freedom is in ourselves. When one's soul is free, then there is nothing in this world that binds one; everywhere one will breathe freedom, in heaven and on earth.

Chapter 10.

THE FREEDOM OF THE SOUL (III)

*Our despair, our depression, our sorrow, our worries
may have innumerable causes. But at the back of all
these is one and the same cause, and that is that our
soul is striving every day for freedom.*

In the East it is said that the reason why an infant cries
immediately after its birth is because it grieves over the loss
it experiences, and this loss is the loss of freedom. The soul,
which was once free, which could float into spheres higher
than the birds, which could expand and live as light and life,
became captive in this limited body of flesh and bones when
it came to earth, a sphere that is quite new and strange to
the infant. Neither has it yet made any connection with
earthly beings or with the earthly atmosphere. That is why
the first thing a soul does is to cry. The Sufis, all mystics,
have recognized this fact and have founded their philosophy
on this theory: that through every condition in life man is
consciously or unconsciously seeking for freedom.

It may be that one is seeking freedom from having to

work; another may be seeking freedom by getting away from some influence which surrounds him; perhaps another seeks freedom from a national point of view. But they each and all strive continually for freedom, and what gives the incentive to strive after freedom is the unconscious craving which the infant feels from the moment of its birth. That is why man is continually striving, knowingly or unknowingly, to attain to that freedom.

Our despair, our depression, our sorrow, our worries may have innumerable causes. But at the back of all these is one and the same cause, and that is that our soul is striving every day for freedom, which is something that perhaps only death will give us. People very often commit suicide hoping they will obtain freedom. Sometimes people think that getting away from everybody will give them this freedom, but they do not know that whatever effort one makes to get out of a situation, one will still not be free, for it is one's own self which is in captivity. Apart from all outward situations which give us the impression of imprisonment, even our own self is captive; we are a captive in ourselves.

The relation between the soul and the body is that of the spark and the charcoal. When the spark of the fire touches the charcoal it is caught by the charcoal. The saying, "It has caught fire," means that the fire, which was apart from it, has been caught by it; and so the soul is caught by the body. One can also look at it in another way; that the body is caught by the soul, or better, that the body is used by the soul. And as the charcoal turns into ashes, so the body in the end is destroyed. But the fire is not lost: it has disappeared to its own element, which is heat.

The sun is in electricity and gaslight and in all forms of heat; it is the sun which manifests through different processes. It is the same with the spirit which, like the sun, has appeared through different processes as souls. One has become many in different forms, although it is not many in reality. Light appears as a fire in a room, or as six or as a hundred different lights, but in reality it is one light. It is only in appearance that each light is limited, because there are so many globes. In the same way each human body has absorbed divine light and shows it as a separate light; and all these lights seen in many globes are called souls. But we may call them the light itself, for it is one spirit seen in different globes as different souls. All human beings are part of one consciousness; they have one source and one goal, although the spirit is caught by different vehicles.

The condition is that the body holds the soul and the soul holds the body. The soul holds the body in order to accomplish its purpose, and the body holds the soul because when the soul leaves it will turn into nothing. Therefore the body is continually striving to keep the soul, because it is made for the soul and lives for it; it is the body's continual desire that the soul should live in it. That being so, it is only when the soul feels it has finished its work and should no longer exist in the body that it leaves the body; or perhaps the body has become so feeble that it can no longer hold the soul. This is the way it happens, and as a result there is death.

Very often there are people who wish to die and do not die. The reason is that it is the mind which wishes death, but the body is still clinging to the soul and the soul is still using the body for its purpose, although the mind is against it; that is why death does not come. Sometimes one thinks that the body is too feeble, that it can no longer hold the soul, and yet the mind says, "I have not finished; I have not seen my friend, or my husband, or my daughter; I would like to live until I see them;" and it goes on living because the soul, having the impression that something is not finished, keeps holding on to that body which can no longer hold the soul. It holds on as long as that particular desire lasts.

After the soul has been caught by the physical body, there comes a time when the soul awakens. As long as it is asleep it is in a kind of dream in the physical body. That is the condition of the average man: a kind of dream. The mystic is the one who is awakened. The amusing thing is that the average man will call the mystic a dreamer, whereas in reality it is he himself who is dreaming! During this dream the soul knows nothing except what appears before it, for instance desires, habits, wishes, experiences, environment, actions, thoughts, and impressions. All these are like a dream which a soul dreams. One person will perhaps dream all his life; there is another who will wake at an early age or in his youth; but there are souls, as in the case of Jesus Christ, who from childhood begin to manifest their awakened condition. Therefore awakening does not depend upon a certain age; even an infant may be awakened. And it may be that a person will live all his life in a dream and may leave this world in the same dream. Though there is a subconscious awakening when something begins to say, "You are dreaming; there is something else for you to know," often one does not listen to it.

But sooner or later that time may come in our lives when we waken from the dream. And as soon as we wake our first thought is, "What is it all about? Why are we here? What are we doing here? Where are we to go? What is the purpose of our life?" And when this thought comes, then a person begins to feel a little less interested in the things of daily life. This does not mean that he is less capable of doing them; on the contrary, an awakened person can accomplish greater worldly things than the one who dreams, and in a better way. If our politicians today, our great merchants and wealthy men, educators and scientists, were spiritual persons, the world would become different; and they themselves would not be any less than they are; indeed they would accomplish greater things.

Do you think if the generals, the politicians, the statesmen and businesspeople of today were awakened souls, we would have had wars? By this time we should be past those days of stupidity when people killed one another; we are in a different stage of evolution, and today there should be no need for war. Humanity is grown up; it is no longer an infant. But even after a war there is no security of peace. We do not know what will happen tomorrow, and that shows that there is something missing. And what is missing is the realization of the dream: people think they are awakened, that they have common sense, and yet they are still asleep. We must be wakened from this dream we are in; the soul must come to the realization of what it is. Then a better day will come for us.

The first sign one notices after the awakening of the soul is that one begins to see from two points of view. One begins to see the right of the wrong and the wrong of the right. One begins to see the good of the bad and the bad of the good. One begins to see that everything is reflected in its opposite. In this way one rises above intellectuality, which then begins to appear as a primitive or elementary knowledge. One sees the dark in the bright and the light in the dark, death in birth and birth in death. It is a kind of double view of things. And when one has reached this, then reason has made way for higher reasoning. No doubt one's language will become gibberish to others; people will not understand it. They will be confused by what one says. To some it will be too simple, to others too subtle: too simple for those who only hear words without meaning, and too subtle for those who strive to understand the meaning and do not reach it.

The third sign is that in failure one will not feel such disappointment, and in success not such a great joy. In adverse conditions one will not be so dejected; in favorable conditions not so conceited. And the continual changes we experience in this world—such as friends turning into enemies, love sometimes turning to hate, sense to senselessness —these little surprises that we experience every day in this world when things are different from what we expected, all these shocks will not be felt so deeply. Life in the world is full of shocks; there is no end to them. At every turn we find some surprise, all the time something new; but when the soul is awakened we do not feel these shocks so deeply. They come, but they do not hit us so heavily.

At the same time, in spite of all this there comes a deeper feeling. An advanced person is more susceptible to hurts than the one who is not advanced, because his heart becomes tender and he feels acutely; he is living. A rock would not feel so. This awakening of the soul gives fineness on one hand and strength to sustain shocks on the other.

And then we come to another stage that develops after the awakening of the soul, and that is the desire for freedom. People think they can attain freedom by retiring from the affairs of the world. No doubt that is a temptation; a spiritual person regards it as temptation. An awakened soul no longer considers the dream important, and yet he will say, "When I retire I shall still work, because I shall still be able to be useful." That is the thought when one is less selfish.

The ultimate freedom of the soul is gained by concentration, by meditation, by contemplation, and by realization. What concentration is needed for the freedom of the soul? The concentration on that object which is prescribed by one's spiritual teacher, so that by the thought of that particular object one may be able to forget oneself for a moment. And then what contemplation is necessary? The contemplation that "This, my limited self, is no longer myself but God's own instrument, God's temple which is made in order that the name of God be glorified." What meditation is required? Meditation on the thought of God, the being of God, forgetting absolutely one's limited self. And the realization is this, that then whatever voice comes to one is God's voice, every guidance is God's guidance, every impulse is a divine impulse, every action is done by God. It is in this way that the soul is made free. And in the freedom of the soul lies the purpose of life.

Chapter 11.

"CRY OUT IN THE NAME OF THY LORD"

... Thus the ultimate purpose for which the soul is seeking every moment of our life is our spiritual purpose.

Every intelligent person comes to a stage in his life, sooner or later, when he begins to question himself as to what purpose there is in life, in being on earth. "Why am I here? What am I to accomplish in life?" he asks. No doubt the moment this question has arisen in a person he has taken his first step in the path of wisdom; before, whatever he did, not being conscious of his life's purpose, he remained discontented. Whatever be his occupation, his condition in life, whether he is wise or foolish, learned or illiterate, there is always discontent. He may have success or failure, but the desire that his life's purpose should be accomplished remains, and unless it is accomplished a person cannot be satisfied. That is why many people who are successful in business, doing very well in their profession, comfortable in their domestic life, and popular in society, yet remain dissatisfied, because they do not know the purpose of their life.

After knowing the purpose of life, we may be handicapped by many things; we may lack means, but the conditions will be favorable to go forward in spite of everything. When someone has found his life's purpose, no matter how difficult life is for him or how many hindrances he has to contend with, from that moment there is nothing he will not withstand, no sacrifice he will not make, nothing he will not endure. He will wait with patience all his life, and if he does not succeed in this life, he will wait even until the hereafter, happy because he is accomplishing his life's purpose. When a person knows, "I am here for this particular purpose," that knowledge in itself gives a great strength of conviction.

There is a story told of the Prophet Muhammad that when the time came that the Prophet, who was born for that particular purpose in life, felt a kind of restlessness, a dissatisfaction with everything in life, he thought he had better go into the forest, into the wilderness, into the mountains, and sit there alone to get in touch with himself, to find out why there was that yearning after something he did not know. He asked his wife if she would allow him the solitude his soul longed for, and she agreed. Then he went into the wilderness and sat there for days together. And when the vibrations of the physical body and mind, which are always upset and in turmoil in the midst of the world, calmed down, and when his mind became quiet and his spirit was tranquil, when the heart of the Prophet became restful, he began to feel in touch with all nature there—the space, the sky, the earth; and then it seemed as if everything was talking to him, as if the water and the clouds were talking. He was in communication with the whole world, with the whole of life.

Then the word came to the Prophet: "Cry out in the name of thy Lord." This is the lesson of idealism: not only being in touch with nature, but idealizing the Lord. In these days there is the great drawback that when people become very intelligent they lose idealism. If they want to find God they want to find Him in figures. There are many who would rather meditate than worship or pray. In this way there has always been conflict between the intellectual person and the idealistic person. The Prophet was taught as the first thing to idealize the Lord; and when the ideal he thus made became his conception of God, then in that conception God awakened. And he began to hear the voice saying, "Now you must serve your people, you must awaken in your people the sense of religion, the ideal of God, the desire for spiritual attainment, and the wish to live a better life." Then he knew that it was now his turn to accomplish all those things that the prophets who had come before had been meant to accomplish.

We are all born in this world to accomplish a certain purpose, and as long as a man does not know this purpose he remains ignorant of life; he cannot call himself a living being. A machine has no choice, it cannot find its life's purpose; but an individual is responsible to a great extent. Very often out of weakness a man gives in to something that otherwise he would have refused to accept. This weakness comes through lack of patience and endurance, lack of self-confidence, and lack of trust. A person who does not trust in providence, who cannot have patience, who cannot endure, will take what comes at the moment; he will not wait until tomorrow. Perhaps the purpose of his life would have opened up before him if he had had more power of endurance, more self-confidence, more trust in providence. But when he possesses none of these things he is just like a machine. He is not pleased with what comes in life, he is grudging every day, he is confused; and yet he goes on like a horse that is not willing to go on, but is yoked to the cart and has to go on. The first knowledge we must gain is the knowledge of the purpose of our life.

It is a great pity that education as it is today pays very little attention to this question. Children, youths, and grown-ups all go through life toiling from morning until evening, studying or working, and at the same time not knowing what purpose they have to accomplish. Among a thousand persons there may be one exception, but nine hundred and ninety-nine are placed in a situation, whether they desire it or not, where they are working just like a mechanism, a machine put in a certain place that is made for it and where it must work. Out of a hundred, perhaps ninety–nine are discontented with the work they are doing. Either it is their environment that has placed them there, or it is because they must work for their living, or because they have the idea that they should first gather what they need. By the time they have gathered the means to be able to do something in life, the desire of accomplishing something is gone.

It is a great drawback that in spite of progress individuals often have no opportunity to accomplish something they desire. Many youths never realize this; they think, "We must do that work and that is all;" and they have no time to think about the purpose of their particular life. Thus hundreds and thousands of lives are wasted. In spite of all the money they make, their hearts are not satisfied, for it is not the wealth one gains that can give that satisfaction.

On hearing from the Prophet that all things and beings were created for a certain purpose, someone said, "O Prophet, I cannot understand why mosquitoes were created!" And the Prophet answered, "They were created so that you may get up quickly at night and engage yourself in prayer!" Everything is created with a purpose, in order that we may use it for its purpose. And so it is with people. Sa'adi says, "Every being is created for a purpose, and the light of that purpose is already kindled in his soul." As we need blacksmiths and goldsmiths and farmers and others, so we need philosophers and mystics and prophets. That creates the harmony, in just the same way as we need sharp and flat in music. If it were not so there would be no beauty, for beauty is created through variety.

When we look at life with a philosopher's view we see that every person is like one note in this symphony of life; that we all make this symphony of life, each contributing the music that is needed in the symphony. But if we do not know our own part in the symphony of life, naturally it is as if one of the four strings on the violin were not tuned, and if it is not tuned it cannot give the music it should produce. So we must each produce that part for which we are born. If we do not contribute what we are meant to and what we should contribute, we are not in tune with our destiny. It is only by playing the particular part that belongs to us that we shall get satisfaction.

Maybe many people will not think as I do, for instance those who believe strongly in pacifism, in the peace ideal. They will say, "Is it not madness that anybody should make a war?" But everything one does, though it may look better or worse, yet belongs somewhere in the scheme of life, and we have no right to condemn it. The principal thing for every individual is to become conscious of the duty for which he is born.

There are in reality two purposes of life. One is the minor, the other is the major purpose of life. One is the preliminary, and the other is the final purpose. The preliminary purpose of life is just like a stepping-stone to the final one. Therefore, one should first consider the preliminary purpose of life.

In the East there are various stories told about sages and saints who have awakened someone to the purpose of his particular life; and the moment that person was awakened, his whole life changed. There is an account in the history of India of the life of Shivaji, who was a young robber who used to attack travelers passing along the way where he lived and rob from them whatever he could. One day before going to his work he came to a sage and greeted him and said, "Sage, I want your blessing, your help in my occupation." The sage asked what his occupation was. He said, "I am an unimportant robber." The sage said, "Yes, you have my blessing." The robber was very pleased, and went away and had greater success than before. Happy with his success, he returned to the sage and greeted him by touching his feet and said, "What a wonderful blessing it is to be so successful." But the sage said, "I am not yet satisfied with your success. I want you to be more successful. Find three or four more robbers and join together and then go on with your work." He joined with four or five other robbers who went with him and again had great success. Once more Shivaji came to the sage and said, "I want your blessing." The sage said, "You have it. But still I am not satisfied. Four robbers are very few. You ought to form a gang of twenty." So he found twenty robbers. And eventually there were hundreds of them.

Then the sage said, "I am not satisfied with the little work you do. You are a small army of young men, and you ought to do something great. Why not attack the Moghul strong-holds and push them out, so that in this country we may reign ourselves?" And so he did, and a kingdom was estab-lished. The next move of the robber would have been to form an empire of the whole country, but he died. Had he lived, Shivaji would have formed an empire. The sage could have said, "What a bad thing, what a wicked thing you are doing. Go in the factory and work!" But the sage saw what Shivaji was capable of. Robbery was his first lesson, his A B C. He had only a few steps to advance to be the defender of his country, and the sage realized that he was going to be a king, to release his people from the Moghuls. The robbers did not see it, and the young man did not think about it. He was pushed into it by the sage. The sage was not pushing him into robbery; he was preparing him for a great work.

Why in the East is the greatest importance given to a teacher in the spiritual path? For this reason: as Hafiz has said, "If your teacher says, 'Sprinkle your prayer rug with wine,' do it." A prayer rug is a holy object; wine is consid-ered unwholesome; but Hafiz continues, "For the knower knows best which way to go." For instance, if a person wishes to collect wealth, his whole mind is absorbed in it. He may be told, "No, that is not a good thing. What is wealth after all? It is unreal, useless. You ought to be devo-tional, spiritual!" But his mind will not be there. He cannot be spiritual. He is concentrated on that particular thing, and because he cannot collect the money he wants, he is unhappy. If one forces upon him spirituality, religion, devotion, prayer, they will not help him. Very often people give water in place of food, and food in place of water. That is not good. Spirituality comes in its time. But the preliminary purpose is what a man will contribute to the world as the first step before awakening to spiritual perfection.

All the great teachers of humanity have taught that preliminary purpose of life in their religions. Whatever teachings they have given to their followers, their motive has been to help them to accomplish the first purpose in life. For instance, when Christ called the fishermen he said, "Follow me, and I will make you fishers of men." He did not say he would make them more spiritual. That was the first step. He wanted them to accomplish the first purpose of life; the next purpose was to become more spiritual. To the teachers of spiritual knowledge who look at it in this way, their first duty is to show someone how to accomplish the first purpose of life. When they have done this, then they show the second purpose.

There are several different ways people take in their lives. One way is the way of material benefit. By profession, by occupation, business, or industry, a person wants to make money. Something is to be said both for and against this ideal. Against it may be said that while working for money one very often loses the right track, thought, and consideration. One easily overlooks the rights of others when one is working for money. And what is to be said for it is this: that it is after all those who possess wealth who can use wealth for the best purpose. All charitable institutions, hospitals, schools, colleges, are raised by charitable people who have given generously to such organizations. There is, therefore, nothing wrong in earning money and in devoting one's time to it, as long as the motive is right and good.

Another aspect is duty. One considers that one has a duty to one's community, town, or country; one does some social work, one tries to do good to others and considers it one's duty. It may be that one has a duty towards one's parents; one may be looking after one's mother and sacrifice one's life for her, or for one's wife or husband and children. There is great merit in this also. No doubt what speaks against it is that very often such lives are spoiled, and they have no chance to do anything worthwhile in the world; but if it were not for the dutiful the world would be devoid of love and affection. If the wife had no sense of duty towards her husband, nor the neighbor towards his friend, then they would be living like creatures of the lower creation. It is the sense of duty that makes man greater than other beings; that is why we admire it. Heroes who give their lives for their country are not doing a small thing. It is something great when a person gives his life for the sake of duty. Besides, duty is a great virtue.

At the time of the last war there was a young woman who was always displeased and in disagreement with her husband, and she was always wanting a separation. When the call to arms came, her husband went to the battlefield, and he hoped that in his absence she would find someone else. As the war went on she thought that while her husband was fighting she would enroll as a nurse. And it happened that near the place where she was working, the husband was wounded; he lost his eyes, and she became his nurse. When she saw him in the condition she was astonished that it had so come about that she was to be his nurse. She had just received a letter containing a proposal of marriage, but she tore it up and changed her mind in an instant; she said, "Now that he has lost his eyes and that he is helpless, I shall remain his wife, I shall take care of him all his life."

Duty, the sense of duty, is a great virtue; and when it is perfected and deepened in the heart of a man it wakens him to a greater and higher consciousness. In that way people have accomplished noble things. The great heroes have lived a life of duty.

The sense of duty comes from idealism. The greater his

ideal of duty, the greater the man. According to the Hindus, the observers of duty are considered religious, because *dharma*, the Sanskrit word which means religion, also means duty.

Another purpose one chooses in life is to make the best of the present. It is the point of view of Omar Khayyám, who told one to "drink the cup of life just now." There is a quatrain in the *Rubayat* in which he says:

> O my Beloved, fill the cup that clears
> Today of past regrets and future fears.
> Tomorrow! why, tomorrow I may be
> Myself with yesterday's sev'n thousand years!

It is the point of view of the person who says, "If I was great in the past, what does it matter? The past is forgotten. And the future—who knows what will come out of it? No one knows his future. Let us make the best of this moment, let us make life as happy as we can." It is not a bad point of view. It is a philosophical point of view. Those who adhere to it are happy and give happiness to others.

No doubt all these different points of view have a wrong side also. But when we look at their right side there is something in it to appreciate.

People nowadays use the phrase, "He is a jolly good fellow." In songs and on different occasions this phrase is used to show appreciation for that tendency of mind that tries to make this moment happy. It is difficult, very difficult, and not everyone can manage to do it; for life has so many conflicts, so many troubles. One has to face so many difficulties in life that to be able to keep on smiling is not everyone's achievement. In order to keep smiling, a person must either be very foolish and not feel or think about anything, but just close both his eyes and his heart to the world, be as high as the souls meant by the story of the miracle of Christ walking upon the water. There are some who sink and some who swim, and others who walk over the water. Those who are drowned in life's misery are those who cannot get out of it, who are tied down in the depths of life and cannot get out, and are miserable there; those are the ones who sink. Then there are others who are swimming; they are those who strive through the conflicting conditions of life in order someday to reach the shore.

There are, however, others who walk upon life. Theirs is the life that is symbolically expressed in the miracle of Christ walking upon the water. It is like living in the world and not being of the world, touching the world and not being touched by it. It needs a clear perception of life, keen intelligence and thorough understanding, together with great courage, strength, and bravery. By this I do not mean to say that the man who makes the best of each present moment is the same as the man whom we call happy-go-lucky, the simple man. That man is the one who lives in another world: he is not aware of life's conditions, he is not awake to the conflicting influences of life. If he is happy it is not surprising, for he is happiness himself. I mean those who are awakened to life's conditions, those who are tender and sensitive to the thoughts and feelings of others. For them it is very difficult to go on living and at the same time to keep smiling. If a man can do it, it is certainly a great thing.

The last aspect is that of those who think, "What is life on earth after all! Is it not only a few days to pass somehow?" The day ends, the months and the years pass, and so time slips by. One comes to the end of life before one has expected it, and the whole past becomes like a dream in the night. Ask a man who has lived a hundred years, "What do you think about life on earth?" He will say, "One night's dream, my child, it is no longer than that."

If that is all there is to life, then those who consider it thus will realize they should think about the hereafter. Just as some think, "While we are able to work we must strive in order to make provision for our old age that we may be more comfortable," those who think of the hereafter say, "Life is short, it is nothing but an opportunity. We must prepare something so that later we shall have the benefit of it." Maybe there will be some who have the right understanding, while others make too much of it and have a wrong conception of the hereafter; yet the wise ones who believe that they must use the time and opportunity that is given to them in this life to prepare for the next one have accomplished a great deal. It is something to admire.

It is said that the earth and the sky and space do not accommodate a person who does not answer life's demands, although for exceptional souls there are exceptional laws, for the lives of exceptional beings cannot be explained in ordinary terms. One may ask what will be the future of those who have not fulfilled the demand of life; will they have to come back to learn their lesson once more? We must all learn our lesson right now. Life is lived right now, its demand is right now, and we must answer it right now. At every moment we are asked to perform a certain duty, to fulfill a certain obligation; and to become conscious of this and to do it in the most fitting and right manner, that is the true religion.

We understand life's demands by understanding life better. There are some who do not answer life's demands because they do not know what life asks of them; and there are others who do not answer life's demands although they do know. When the demands of the outer life are different from what the inner life asks of us, we should fulfill the demands of the outer life without neglecting those of the inner life, as it is said in the Bible: "Render unto Caesar the things that are Caesar's, and unto God the things that are God's."

We have to become like the ebb and flow. This is a symbolical expression. A certain thing is accomplished at one time by sympathy, and at another time by indifference; one situation we must meet by taking interest in it, in another situation we must become indifferent, not concerned with it. If in a sea there were always ebb and no flow, or always flow and no ebb, then this would be a dead sea. The living sea is both inhaling and exhaling; thus in everything we do in life, we should be able to meet every situation and event with the manner that the situation demands.

These are the four different ways people take in order to accomplish the purpose of their lives: making wealth, being conscientious in their duty, making the best of every moment of life, and preparing for the future. All these four have their good points. And once one realizes this, there is no need to blame anyone for having taken another path than our own for the accomplishment of life's purpose. By understanding this, one becomes tolerant.

And now we come to the ultimate purpose of life, which is always one and the same: for every man has in the end to accomplish the same purpose, in whatever way he will. He will come to it either consciously or unconsciously, easily or with difficulty; but he has to accomplish it. That purpose is spiritual attainment. One might wonder if a person who is so material that he never thinks about it, and who refuses to consider this question, will ever attain to spiritual realization, but the answer is yes; everyone, consciously or unconsciously, is striving after spiritual attainment. Sometimes one does not take the same way as we do, sometimes his point of view and his method differ, and sometimes one person attains to spiritual realization much sooner than another. It may be reached in a day, and another person may have striven for it all his life and yet not have attained it. What determines this? It is the evolution of a particular soul.

There are stories told in India of how a person was awakened to spiritual consciousness after hearing one word from his guru. That one word inspired him instantly to touch the higher consciousness. And then again we hear the stories in the East of people who went to the forest or to the mountains, who fasted for days and months, who were hanging by their feet, their head downwards, or who stood erect for years and years. This shows how difficult it is for one person and how easy for another. We make a great mistake today when we consider every man's evolution as the same. There are great differences between people. One is creeping, one is walking, one is running, and another is flying. And yet they all live under the same sun.

It is the custom in the East for those who begin to seek for a spiritual purpose to look for a spiritual teacher. They do not set forth on the spiritual journey by themselves, for thousands of years of experience have taught that to tread the spiritual path it is necessary to have some leader to whom one can give one's confidence and trust in order to follow him to the end. No doubt in the West there is a general awakening. Everyone wishes to know something about the spiritual path; but the difficulty is that everyone does not stick to one and the same thing. There are many who will go first to one esoteric school and then to another, and so on. In the end they have learned so much that they do not know what is true and what is false, which is right and which is wrong. It is just like visiting a restaurant and eating so much that one is not able to digest it. Besides, when a person takes in all that is false and true, there remains no discrimination between false and true.

To realize the preliminary purpose of our life, we must find our natural rhythm. Today people adopt wrong methods. They go to a clairvoyant and ask him about the purpose of their life. They do not know it themselves. Anybody else must tell them except their own spirit, their own soul; they ask others because they do not tune themselves to that pitch where they can feel intuitively what they live for. If another person says, "You are here to become a carpenter or a lawyer or a barrister," that does not satisfy our need. It is our own spirit that must speak to us. We must be able to still ourselves, to tune our spirit to the universal consciousness, in order to know the purpose of our life. And once we know this purpose, the best thing is to pursue it in spite of all difficulties. Nothing should discourage us, nothing should keep us back once we know that this is the purpose of our life. Then we must go after it even at the sacrifice of everything, for when the sacrifice is great, the gain in the end gives a greater power and a greater inspiration. Rise or fall, success or failure does not matter as long as you know the purpose of your life. If ninety-nine times you fail, the hundredth time you will succeed.

Thus the ultimate purpose for which the soul is seeking every moment of our life is our spiritual purpose. You may ask how to attain to that purpose. The answer is that what you are seeking is within yourself. Instead of looking outside, you must look within. The way to proceed to accomplish this is for some moments to suspend all your senses, such as sight, hearing, smell, and touch, in order to put a screen before the outside life; and by concentration and by developing that meditative quality, you will sooner or later get in touch with the inner self, which is more communicative and speaks more loudly than all the noises of this world; and this gives joy, creates peace, and produces in you a self-sufficient spirit, a spirit of independence and of true liberty. The moment you get in touch with your self you are in communion with God. It is in this way, if God-communication is sought rightly, that spirituality is attained.

Chapter 12.

EVEN IN THE BREAKING OF THE HEART

In the consciousness of perfection lies the purpose of this whole manifestation.

If a Sufi is asked what was the purpose of this creation, he will say that the Knower, the only Knower, wanted to know Himself, and there was only one condition of knowing Himself, which was to make Himself intelligible to His own Being. For Intelligence itself is a Being, but Intelligence is not known to itself. Intelligence becomes known to itself when there is something intelligible. Therefore, the Knower had to manifest Himself, thus becoming an object to be known. And by this knowledge the Knower arrives at perfection. It does not mean that the Knower lacked perfection, for all perfection belonged to the Knower; only He became conscious of His perfection. Therefore, it is in the consciousness of perfection that lies the purpose of this whole manifestation.

The Sufis say, "God is love." That is true, but the love was not sufficient. The love had to make an object to love in order to see its own nature, to experience its own character, to fathom its own mystery, to find its own joy. For instance, the seed has in it the leaf and the flower and the fruit; but the fulfillment of the purpose of that seed is that it is put in the ground, that it is watered, that a seedling springs up and is reared by the sun; it brings forth its flowers and fruits. This is the fulfillment of that seed, which already contained in itself the fruit and flower. A person who does not see the reason of all this is in the seed state; his mind is in the state of a seed that has not yet germinated, that has not yet produced its seedling and has not yet experienced the springing of the plant.

No sooner does the soul begin to unfold and experience in life the purpose that is hidden within itself than it begins to feel the joy of it; it begins to value the privilege of living; it begins to appreciate everything; it begins to marvel at everything. For in every experience, good or bad, it finds a certain joy, and that joy is in the fulfillment of life's purpose. That joy is not only experienced in pleasure but even in pain, not only in success but also in failures; not only in the cheerfulness of the heart but even in the breaking of the heart there is a certain joy hidden. For there is no experience that is worthless; and especially for that soul who is beginning to realize this purpose, there is no moment wasted in life. For under all circumstances and in all experiences that soul is experiencing the purpose of life.

This may be understood by a little example. A djinn wanted to amuse himself, but when about to do so, he brought upon himself a problem. For the djinn was powerful, and he said to himself, "Be thou a rock"; and the djinn turned into a rock. But by becoming a rock he began to feel solitary, and left in the wilderness he felt the loss of action, loss of movement, lack of freedom and lack of experience. This was a terrible captivity for the djinn. For many years this djinn had to have patience to be able to change into something else. It did not mean that through the rock he did not realize life. For even the rock is living, even the rock is changing, and yet a rock is a rock; a rock is not a djinn. It was through the patience of thousands of years that the rock began to wear out and crumble into earth. And when, out of that earth, the djinn came out as a plant, he was delighted that he had grown out as a tree. The djinn was so pleased to find that out of a rock he could become a plant, that he could enjoy the air more fully, that he could swing in the wind. He smiled at the sun and bathed happily in the rain. He was pleased to bring forth fruits, to bring forth flowers.

But at the same time his innate desire was not satisfied. It kept him hoping some day to break through this captivity of being rooted in a particular place and of this limitation of movement. For a long, long time the djinn was waiting to come out of this limitation. This was better, yet it was not the experience the djinn desired. But at last the fruit became decayed and part of that fruit turned into a little worm. The djinn was even more delighted to feel that he could move about and was now no longer rooted to one place and unable to move. And as this worm breathed and was in the sun, it grew wings and began to fly. The djinn was still more delighted to see that he could do this. He flew through the air and experienced the life of a bird, now sitting upon the trees, now walking on the earth. And as he enjoyed life on the earth more and more, he became a heavy bird. He could not fly; he walked. And this heaviness made him coarse, and he turned into an animal. He was most happy, for then he could oppose all the other animals that wanted to kill birds, because he was no longer a bird.

Through a process of gradual change, the djinn arrived at the point of becoming man. And when he became a man, the djinn looked around and thought, "This is something that I was destined to be. Because now, as a djinn, I can see all these different bodies that I have taken in order to become more free, to become perceptive and sensitive, to know things, and to enjoy things more fully. There could not have been any vehicle more fitting than this." And yet he thought, "Even this is not a fitting vehicle, because when I want to fly I have no wings, and I feel like flying also. I walk on the earth, but I have not the strength of the lion. And now I feel that I belong to heaven, and where it is I don't know." This made the djinn search for what was missing, until in the end he realized. "I was a djinn just the same, in the rock, in the plant, in the bird, in the animal; but I was captive and my eyes were veiled from my own being. It is by becoming man that I am now beginning to see that I was a djinn. And yet I also find in this life of man a great limitation, for I have not that freedom of expression, that freedom of movement, that life that is dependable, that knowledge that is reality." And then this thought itself took him to his real domain, which was the djinn life; and there he arrived with the air of the conqueror, with the grandeur of the sovereign, with the splendor of a king, with the honor of an emperor, and realizing, "After all, I have enjoyed myself, I have experienced though I have suffered, I have known being, and I have become what I am."

The Knower manifested as man in order that He might become known to Himself; and now, what may man do in order to help the Knower to fulfill this purpose? Seek continually an answer to every question that arises in his heart. Of course, there are different types of minds. There may be one person whose mind will puzzle and puzzle over a question, and who will trouble himself for something that is nothing, and will go out by the same door by which he has come in. That person will trouble himself and will wreck his own spirit, and will never find satisfaction. There is no question that has not its answer somewhere. The answer is nothing but an echo of the question, a full echo. And therefore one must rise above this confused state of mind, which prevents one from getting the answer, from within or from without, to every question that arises in one's heart. In order to become spiritual, one need not perform miracles. The moment one's heart is able to answer every question that rises in one's heart, one is already on the path. Besides, the thing that must be first known, one puts off to the last, and that which must be known at the last moment one wants to know first. It is this that causes confusion in the lives of many souls.

The words of Christ support this argument: "Seek ye first the kingdom of God, and all these things will be added unto you." This is the very thing one does not want to seek; one wishes to find anything else but this. And where is it to be found? Not in the knowledge of another person, but in the knowing of self. If a person goes through his whole life most cleverly judging others, he may go on, but he will find himself to be more foolish at every step; at the end he reaches the fullness of stupidity. But the one who tries, tests, studies and observes himself—his own attitude in life, his own outlook on life, his thought, speech and action—who weighs and measures and teaches himself self-discipline, is the person who is able to understand another better. How rarely one sees a soul who concerns himself with himself through life, in order to know! Mostly, every soul seems to be busily occupied with the lives of others. And what do they know in the end? Nothing. If there is a kingdom of God to be found anywhere, it is within oneself.

And it is, therefore, in the knowledge of self that the fulfillment of life lies. The knowledge of self means the knowledge of one's body, the knowledge of one's mind, the knowledge of one's spirit; the knowledge of the spirit's relation to the body and the body's relation to the spirit; the knowledge of one's wants and needs, the knowledge of one's virtues and faults; knowing what we desire and how to attain it, what to pursue and what to renounce. And when one dives deep into this, one finds before one a world of knowledge that never ends. And it is that knowledge that gives one insight into human nature and brings one to the knowledge of the whole of creation, and in the end, one attains to the knowledge of the divine Being.

Chapter 13.

TO HOLD LOVE'S FLAME HIGH

If God is love, love is most sacred, and to utter this word
without meaning is a vain repetition.

The purpose of life, in short, is that the only Being makes
His oneness intelligible to Himself. He goes through different planes of evolution, or planes through which He arrives
at different changes, in order to make clear to Himself His
oneness. And as long as this purpose is not accomplished,
the one and only Being has not reached His ultimate satisfaction, in which lies His divine perfection. One may ask, "Is
man the only organ through which God realizes His oneness?" God realizes His oneness through His own nature.
Since God is one, He always realizes His oneness through all
things; through man He realizes His oneness in its fullness.
For instance, in the tree there are many leaves; although each
leaf is different from each other leaf, yet the difference is not
great. Then, coming to worms and germs and birds and
animals, they are different one from another, and yet the
difference is not so distinct as in man. And when one thinks

77

of the great variety of the numberless human forms, and it seems that there is not one form exactly like another, this by itself gives us a living proof of the oneness of God. In order to show this, Asaf Nizam made a very beautiful verse: "You look at me with contempt. Yes, granted; I am contemptible. But will you show me such another contemptible creature?" Which means: even the worst person is incomparable; there is none like him. It is a great phenomenon, and the proof of oneness, the proof of unity, that in the creation of God there is no competition, no one competes with the Creator. In other words, it would be unworthy if the only Being felt, "There is another like Me, even in the world of variety." He retains His pride even in the world of variety: "No one is like Me." Even in the worst guise He stands alone without comparison. One may ask, "Before man appeared on earth, did God realize His oneness?" But who can say how many times man appeared on earth and disappeared from the earth? What we know is only one history of the planet. But how many planets exist? In how many millions of years have how many creations been created and how many withdrawn? All one can say is this: one cannot speak of God's past, present, and future; one can only give an idea that is the central idea of all aspects of truth that it is the only Being who existed, who exists and who will exist and all that we see are His phenomena.

There is a story that can explain the mystery of life's purpose. A fairy had a great desire to amuse herself, and she descended on the earth. And there children had made a little doll's house. She wanted to enter this doll's house, but it was difficult for her to enter into the space where only a doll could go. "Very well" she said, "I am going to try a different way. I will send one finger by this way, and another finger by another way, and each part by different ways." And she separated into different bits, and each bit of herself went through the different parts of the doll's house. And when one part met the other part, at once they rubbed against one another, and that was very unpleasant. And there was a fight among the different parts: "Why are you coming my way? this was my way; why do you come my way?" Each part of the fairy's being interested itself in something, in some part of that doll's house. When that moment of interest passed, a certain part of her being wanted to go out of the doll's house. But then there were other parts of the being that were not willing to let it go. They were holding it: "You stay here; you cannot go out." Some parts of her being wanted to push out another part, but there was no way of putting it out. So it was a kind of chaos all through, one part not knowing that the other part belonged to the same fairy, and yet one part being attracted unconsciously to another part because they were parts of the same body. In the end, the heart of the fairy moved about also. This heart soothed every other part, saying, "You have come from me. I wish to console, I wish to serve you. If you are troubled, I wish to take away your trouble. If you are in need of a service, I wish to render it you. If you lack anything, I wish to bring it for you. I know how much you are troubled in this doll's house." But some said, "We are not troubled at all; we are enjoying ourselves. If we are troubled, it is by the wish to remain here. Those who are troubled are others, not we." The heart said, "Well, I shall look at you, and I shall enjoy myself too. I shall sympathize with those who are troubled, I shall help those who are enjoying themselves." This was the one part of the fairy's being that was conscious of its atoms scattered all around. But the atoms were hardly conscious of it, although since they belonged to the same body, they were attracted to the heart, knowingly or unknowingly, consciously or unconsciously. Such was the power of the heart. It was just like the power of the sun, that turns the responsive flower into a sunflower. And so the power of the heart of the fairy turned every part of its being that responded into a heart. And as the heart was light and life itself, the doll's house could no longer hold the heart. The heart was experiencing the joy of the doll's house, but was at the same time able to fly away. The heart was delighted to find all its atoms belonging to its body, and it worked through all and through every part of its organs; so, in time, it turned every part of its organs into a heart als' by which this phenomenon was fulfilled.

God is love. If God is love, love is most sacred, and to utter this word without meaning is a vain repetition. The lips of a person to whom it means something are closed; he can say little. For love is a revelation in itself: no study is necessary, no meditation is needed, no piety is required. If love is pure, if the spark of love has begun to glow, then there is no need to go somewhere to gain spirituality; then spirituality is within. One must keep blowing the spark until it turns into a perpetual fire. The fire-worshippers of old did not worship a fire that went out; they worshipped a perpetual fire. Where is that perpetual fire to be found? In one's own heart. The spark that one finds glowing for a moment and that then becomes dim does not belong to heaven, for in heaven all things are lasting; it must belong to some other place. Love has become a word from the dictionary, a word that is used a thousand times in the day, which means nothing. To the one who knows what it means, love means patience, love means endurance, love means tolerance, love means sacrifice, love means service. All things such as gentleness, humility, modesty, graciousness, kindness; all are the different manifestations of love. It is the same to say, "God is all and all is God," as to say, "Love is all and all is love." And it is to find it, to feel it, to experience its warmth, to see in the world the light of love, to keep its glow, and to hold love's flame high as a sacred torch to guide one in one's life's journey to fulfill the purpose of life. According to the common standard of life, a man with common sense is counted to be a right and a fit person. But by a mystical standard, that person alone can begin to be right who is beginning to feel sympathy with his fellow man. For by the study of philosophy and mysticism, by the practices of concentration and meditation, to what do we attain? To a capability that enables us to serve our fellow human beings better.

Truth is simple. But for the very reason that it is simple, people will not take it—because our life on earth is such that for everything we value, we have to pay a great price, and one wonders, "If truth is the most precious of all things, then how can truth be attained simply?" It is this illusion that makes everyone deny simple truth and seek for complexity. Tell people about something that makes their heads whirl around and around and around. Even if they do not understand it, they are most pleased to think, "It is something substantial; it is something lofty." But something every soul knows, proving what is divine in every soul, and which it cannot help but know, that appears to be too cheap, for the soul already knows it. There are two things: knowing and being. It is easy to *know* truth, but most difficult to *be* truth. It is not in *knowing* truth that life's purpose is accomplished; life's purpose is accomplished in *being* truth.

Chapter 14.

THERE WILL COME A DAY OF AWAKENING

*Each atom of the universe is meant to struggle and strive
in order to become perfect one day.*

The rocks, the trees, the animals, and man, all in their turn,
show an inclination to seek perfection. The tendency of
rocks is to form into mountains reaching upward; and the
waves are ever reaching upward as if they were trying to
attain something that is beyond their reach. The tendency
of birds is the same. Their joy is flying in the air and going
upward. The tendency of many animals is to stand on their
hind legs; and man, who is the culmination of creation, has
from infancy this tendency to stand up. An infant who is not
yet able to stand moves his little hands and legs, showing the
desire to do so.

This all shows the desire for perfection. The law of gravitation is only half known to the world of science, which
believes that the earth attracts all that belongs to it. It is true.
But the spirit also attracts all that belongs to it, and that

other side to the law of gravitation has always been known to the mystics. The law of gravitation is working from two sides: from the side of the earth, which draws all that belongs to the earth, and from the side of the spirit, which attracts the soul towards it. Even those who are unconscious of this law of gravitation are also striving for perfection, for the soul is being continually drawn towards the spirit. They are striving for perfection just the same. In the small things of everyday life a man is never satisfied with what he has; he always wants more and more, be it a higher rank, wealth, or fame. He is always striving for this.

This shows that the heart is like a magic bowl; however much you pour into it, it only becomes deeper; it is always found to be empty. The reason why man is never satisfied is that he is unconsciously striving for perfection; but those who strive consciously after perfection have a different way. Nevertheless, each atom of the universe is meant to struggle and strive in order to become perfect one day. In other words, if a seer happens to be in the mountains, he will hear the mountains cry continually, "We are waiting for that day when something in us will awaken. There will come a day of awakening, of unfoldment; we are silently awaiting it." If he went into the forest and saw the trees standing there they would tell him that they too were waiting patiently. One can feel it; the more one sits there the more one feels that the trees are waiting for the time when there will be an unfoldment. So it is with all beings, but man is so absorbed in his everday actions and his greed that he seems to be unaware of that innate desire for unfoldment. It is his everyday tasks, his avariciousness, his cruelty to other beings, that keep him continually occupied, and that is why he cannot hear the continual cry of his own soul to awaken, to unfold, to reach upward, to expand, and to go towards perfection.

It is the nature of God to wish to realize His own perfection. An artist wishes to bring out the best that is in him: therein lies his satisfaction. In every soul there is a longing to bring out, to bring to a culmination, what is waiting within. And as soon as it has realized this longing, the purpose of that soul's birth on earth has been fulfilled.

As is the nature of the creatures, so is the nature of the Creator. His satisfaction also lies in the realization of perfection. It was to this end that everyting was created by going through this entire process His nature was perfected, and therein lies the fulfillment of His own desire.

All that is in our nature is in the nature of God. The only difference is that God is great and we are small; we are limited and God is unlimited; we represent imperfection, God represents perfection. As we sleep, God sleeps too; if we can be unconscious, there is also God's unconsciousness. It is said in the Bible that man was created in God's image. If one wishes to study God, one must study man.

Is it possible for man to reach perfection? When one sees how limited man is, one can never believe that he is entitled to perfection. There is no end to his limitations, and he cannot even comprehend what perfection means. One becomes pessimistic when it is a question of perfection. Yet we read in the Bible the words of Christ, "Be ye perfect even as your Father in heaven is perfect"; this shows that here is indeed a possibility of perfection. All philosophies and all religious and sacred teachings are intended to bring about that realization that is called perfection. Any philosophy or religion that does not show this path to perfection has been corrupted and fails; there is something missing in it. But if we look at religion as one and the same religion in all the ages, given by different masters of humanity yet inspired by one and the same Spirit of guidance, one and the same light of wisdom, we see that they have all given the same truth. It is only when it is interpreted to suit people of different ages, periods, and races that it varies. But the underlying truth of all religions is one and the same, and whenever a preacher teaches that perfection is not for man, he corrupts the teaching that is given in all the religions; he has not understood it. He professes a certain religion, but he does not understand it, for the main object of every religion is the striving toward perfection.

Many people seeking knowledge say, "What we want in the world today is greater harmony, greater peace, better conditions. We don't want spiritual perfection." But Christ has said in the Bible, "Seek ye first the kingdom of God, and all these things shall be added unto you." The tendency of every man is to seek everything else first and to keep the kindom of God for the last. That which should be sought first is left to the last, and that is why humanity is not evolving towards perfection.

Occupations such as war and preparation for war cannot be called civilized occupations. It is a pity that in this period of civilization man should have wars; and yet we think that we are more civilized than the people of ancient times! Ages before Christ, Buddha taught, *"Ahimsa paramo dharma ha"* —harmlessness is the essence of religion. And he taught people to be friendly even to the smallest insect; he taught them the brotherhood of all things. And we occupy ourselves with wars! Under the conditions existing today we can expect war anywhere in the world. Why is this so? It all comes from seeking perfection in the wrong way. Instead of seeking spiritual perfection, people seek earthly perfection, but what the earth holds is limited, and when everyone struggles for earthly perfection the earth will not be able to answer their demands. Whether we get what we want or not, there will be a continuous struggle.

The main way of seeking for perfection is through religion. Religion has five different aspects, and its principal aspect and foundation is belief in God. What is God? To many the thought of a personal God does not appeal, though they might accept the idea of an abstract God. But they forget that something abstract cannot be a living being. You cannot call something abstract, like space, God. Space is space. You can neither call space God, nor can you call time God. Space is a conception of our own, and in the same way time is a conception. In reality they do not exist.

What is unlimited cannot be comprehended, and what cannot be comprehended is nameless. We can give a name to what is intelligible; if it is unintelligible we cannot give it a name, because we do not know it. And when we consider those who believe in a personal God, we find that many of them merely believe in a certain law given in the name of God; they do good works for the sake of God, but at the same time they only know that there is a God somewhere.

Neither of these types of believer in God has a conception of the real meaning of the God-ideal. They merely have belief in God, and this does not take one much further. The God-ideal is in reality a stepping-stone towards the knowledge of spiritual perfection. It is through the God-ideal that higher knowledge can be gained. And those who wait to see if they will be shown a God before their eyes, or who want a proof of the being of God, are mistaken. That which cannot be compared, which cannot be named, cannot be shown.

For instance, you see light. Light is intelligible to you because there is darkness opposed to it. Things are known by their opposites. Since God has no opposite, God cannot be known in the same way that the things of the earth can be known. Besides, to explain God is to dethrone God; the less said the better; and yet the knowledge of God is necessary for those who seek after perfection.

Different religions have different conceptions of God; but not only the religions, every man has his own conception of God. We cannot think of any being without making a conception in our mind of that being. For instance, if someone told us a fairy tale, the first thing we would do would be to make a conception of a fairy—what it looks like. If someone talks to us about an angel, we make a conception of it. It is a natural tendency to make a conception according to one's own experience and therefore very near to one's own self. A human being does not think of an angel or a fairy as being like a bird or an animal, but as something like himself. If this is true, then it is not a fault when someone has his own idea of God. But it is a great fault on the part of those who want to take away that idea and wish to give that person another idea. It is not right. No one can give to another his own conception of God, because each one must make it real for himself. The prophets of all ages have given some ideal to help man to form a conception of God. It has been said, "If you have no God, make one." That is the right way and the easiest way of realizing the unlimited truth.

In the story about Leila and Majnun—the eastern Romeo and Juliet—someone said to Majnun, the young lover, "Leila is not beautiful. What is she? Why do you love her so much?" And Majnun said humbly, "In order to see Leila you must borrow Majnun's eyes." The conception of God is different and distinct for every person, and one cannot give one's conception of God to another.

There is another story told about a housewife who was preparing a great feast. When her husband came home he said, "My good wife, why have you prepared a feast? It is a birthday? What is it?" She said, "It is more than a birthday, it is a great day for me." But he insisted, "What is it?" She replied, "My husband, I never thought that you believed in God." He asked, "And how did you find out?" She said, "While turning over in sleep you uttered the name of God, and I am so thankful. He said, "Alas. That which was so sacred and secret in my heart has today been revealed. I can no longer sustain it and live." And he dropped down dead. His conception of God was too sacred for him.

There is outer expression and inner expression, and we do not always know which is which. We may think many people are far removed from the God-ideal when they are in fact much nearer to God than ourselves. It is difficult for anyone to judge who is near to God and who is not. It is difficult to know even in our own lives what pleases our friend and what does not please him. The more conscientious we are in wanting to please our friend, the more we find how difficult it is to know what will please him and what will not. Not everyone knows it, but then the light of friendship has not been kindled in everyone. Sometimes it remains a word in the dictionary. One who has learned friendship has learned religion; the one who has learned friendship has attained spiritual knowledge. The one who has learned friendship need learn very little else; morals in Persian are called friendship.

When we cannot understand the pleasure and displeasure of our own friends in this world, how can we understand the pleasure and displeasure of God? Who on earth can say that God is pleased with this or that? No one could ever have the power of making rules and laws, saying God is pleased with this or displeased with that.

Another aspect of religion is the aspect of the teacher. For instance, Christ. There are those who see divinity in Christ. They say, "Christ was God, Christ is divine." And there are others who say, "Christ was a man, one like all of us." When we come to look at this question, we see that the man who says, "Christ is divine" is not wrong. If there is any divinity shown it is in the human being. And the one who says, "Christ was a man," is not wrong either. In the garb of man, Christ manifested. Those who do not want Christ to be a man drag down the greatness and sacredness of the human being by their argument, by saying that man is made of sin and by separating Christ from humanity. But there is nothing wrong in calling Christ man or divine. It is in the human being that divine perfection is to be seen. It is in the human being that divinity is manifested. There are Christ's own words "I am Alpha and Omega." Many close their eyes to this, but the one who said, "I am Alpha and Omega" existed also before the coming of Jesus, and the one who says, "first and last," must exist also after Jesus.

In the words of Christ there is the idea of perfection. He identified himself with that spirit of which he was conscious. Christ was conscious not of his human part but of his perfect being when he said, "I am Alpha and Omega." He did not identify himself here with his being known as Jesus. He identified himself with that spirit of perfection that lived before Jesus and will continue to live to the end of the world, for eternity. If this is so, then what does it matter if some say, "Buddha inspired us," and millions are inspired by Buddha? It is only a difference of name. It is all Alpha and

Omega. If others say Moses, or Muhammad, or Krishna, what difference does it make? Where did the inspiration come from? Was it not from one and the same spirit? Was it not the same Alpha and Omega of which Jesus Christ was conscious? Whoever gives the message to the world, whatever illuminated human beings have raised thousands and millions of people in the world, they cannot but be that same Christ whom the one calls by this name and the other by another name. Yet human ignorance always causes wars and disasters on account of different religions, and different communities, because of the importance they give to their own conception, their own corrupted conception, which differs from another. Even now, on the one hand there is materialism and on the other there is bigotry. What is neccessary today is to find the first and last religion, to come to the message of Christ, to divine wisdom, so that we may recognize wisdom in all its different forms, in whatever form it has been given to humanity. It does not matter if it is Buddhism, Islam, Judaism, Zoroastrianism, or Hinduism. It is one wisdom, that call of the spirit awakens man to rise above limitation and to reach perfection.

The third aspect of religion is the manner of worship. There have been many in different ages who have worshipped the sun, but they have believed in God just the same. The sun was only a symbol. They thought, "This is a light that does not depend upon oil or anything else, something that remains." And then there were others who worshipped sacred trees and holy places, rocks and mountains of ancient traditions; and again others who worshipped heroes of great repute or teachers and masters of humanity. Nevertheless, all had a divine ideal, and the form in which they worshipped does not matter.

The Arabs in desert, where there was no house, no building to go to, stood in the open air and bowed low in the open space at sunset and sunrise. It was all worship of God; it was given in that form. The Hindus made idols of different kinds in order to help man to focus his mind on particular objects.

These were all different prescriptions given by the doctors of souls. They were not pagans or heathens; they were only taught differently by the wise; different thoughts, different ways were given to them just as a doctor would give different prescriptions to different patients in order to obtain the same cure. Therefore, difference in worship does not make a different religion. Religion is one and the same in spite of a thousand different kinds of worship.

The fourth aspect is the moral aspect. Different religions have taught different moral principles; but at the same time there is one human, moral principle on which all is based, and that is justice. And this does not mean justice in principle and in rules and regulations, it means that one, true, religious law that is in man, that is awakened in man. As his soul unfolds itself, this law becomes more and more clear to him: what is just and what is unjust. The most wonderful thing about this law is that a thief or a wicked or unrighteous man may be most unjust to others, but if someone is unjust to him he will say, "He is not just to me." This shows that he, too, knows justice. When he is dealing with others he forgets it, but when it comes to himself he knows justice very well. We are all responsible to ourselves according to that religious law. If we do not regard it, it naturally results in unhappiness; everything that goes wrong does so for the one reason that we do not listen to ourselves.

The fifth aspect of religion is self-realization. This is the highest aspect, and everything we do leads to it: prayers, concentration, good actions, good thoughts. And how is it gained? Some say that we realize God by self-realization. But it is not so, for we can only realize self by the realization of God. Whenever someone tries to realize self while omitting God, he makes a mistake.

It is very difficult for man to realize his true self, because the self he knows is a most limited self. The self to which he is awakened for the time of birth, the self that has made within him a conception of himself, is most limited. However proud and conceited he may be, however good his idea of himself, yet in his innermost being he knows his limitation, the smallness of his being. He may be a most successful general, he may be a king; but he discovers his limitation when the time comes for him to lose his kingdom. Then he knows that he is not really a king. Earthly greatness does not make him great. If there is anything that can make him great, it is only the effacing of himself and the establishing of God instead. The one who wants to begin with self-realization may have many intellectual and philosophical principles, but he will get into a muddle and arrive nowhere. These are wrong methods.

There are people who say, "I am God." This is insolence, stupidity; it is foolish to say such things. They insult the greatest ideal that the prophets and saviors of humanity have always respected. Such people can never reach spiritual perfection. In order to reach spiritual perfection, the first thing is to destroy this false self. First this delusion must be destroyed; and this is done by the ways taught by the great teachers, ways of concentration and meditation, by the power of which one forgets oneself and removes one's consciousness from oneself—in other words, rises from one's limited being. In this way a person effaces himself from his own consciousness, and places God in his consciousness instead of his limited self. And it is in this way that he arrives at the perfection that every soul is seeking.

Chapter 15.

EXCEPT A MAN BE BORN AGAIN

The journey begins with a path of thorns, and the traveler must go barefoot.

There are two different stages in human evolution; the minor and the major stage. In the Hindu Puranic symbology, characters belonging to one or the other of these stages are called the younger and the elder brother.

Just as there is a stage of childhood when the child only knows what it wants and is only happy when it gets it, no matter what might be the consequences, so the minor stage of the soul occurs when man only desires what he can see, hear, perceive, or touch, and beyond that does not care and does not wish for anything else. The major stage occurs when man has experienced life to a certain extent, has known pleasure and pain, enthusiasm and disappointment, and has realized the variability of life; only then has he reached the stage of majority.

These minor and major stages do not depend upon the attainment of a certain age, nor do they depend upon a particular education: they depend upon the inner life. When a man has penetrated into life as far as he can go, and when he has passed the limit of the minor stage, then he arrives at the major stage. In the East there is a custom that has become a kind of religious etiquette: not to wake a person who is asleep. In other words, one should treat the world according to nature and not go against nature. The man who is in the minor stage should not be forced into the major stage; he must first sleep well before he can awake.

On the spiritual path, the man who is in the minor stage says, "Yes, I would like to go on this path, but where shall I arrive?" Before he travels on this path he wants to know all about it. He wants to know whether his friends are going with him, and if they are not, he is not ready to go either. For he is not sure of the way; he will not go alone and wants to know when and where he will arrive, and whether it is safe to journey on that particular path. On his journey, he looks back and at the same time tries to look forward, asking, "Shall I reach the goal? Is it really the right path?" A thousand times doubt comes, or fear; he looks back, forward, around. If others could only tell him how far he has journeyed! He is restless; he wants to know how far he is from the goal. He really is still a child, although he has a desire to travel on. To him the mystical hints for mental research are toys that keep him busy looking at the map of the journey to see where he is going.

About the conditions of the major stage the Bible says, "Except a man be born again he cannot see the kingdom of God." If I were asked what the journey really is, and what is its object, I would answer that the purpose of the whole of creation was for this journey, and that if it were not for this purpose there would be no creation at all. Before a person starts upon this journey, he practices it in some form or other in play, although in reality he has not yet started. For instance, a person desires to be rich, and he devotes all his time and energy, his life and his thoughts, to that object, and, so to speak, journeys towards that goal. If he desires power he makes for that and gets it; if he wants position he uses all his strength to reach that goal. But he does all this in play; and the proof of this is that every time he attains the object he desired and of which he was in pursuit, it only gives him the desire for something else. If he is rich he wants to be famous; if he is famous he wants something else; if he has one thing he strives for another and is never satisfied. It shows that man, outwardly busy in the pursuit of worldly things, is not satisfied, but has a constant yearning in his soul for something more; and this keeps him uneasy. Rumi gives a good explanation of this in his *Masnavi* where he says, "What is it in the reed flute that appeals to your soul, that goes through you, pierces the heart?" And the answer is, it is the crying of the flute, and the reason of its crying is that it once belonged to a plant from which it was cut apart. Holes were made in its heart. It longs to be reunited with its source, with its origin. In another place in his book Rumi says, "So it is with everyone who has left his original country for a long time; he may roam about and feel very pleased with what he sees, but there will come a moment when a strong yearning rises in his heart for the place where he was born."

One sees that those in the world who have really suffered, who have been disappointed, who are broken-hearted, do not wish to tell anybody about their experiences; they do not want any company, but wish to be alone. And then it is as if there were someone waiting with open arms, waiting for such a soul to come as a child comes to its mother. This shows that there is somewhere a consoler greater than any in the world, a friend dearer that anyone else, a protector stronger than any earthly one. Knowing that the world is not to be depended upon, the one who has gone through all this looks for that great one in himself.

The friend who is a friend in life and after death, in pleasure and pain, in riches and poverty, one upon whom one can always depend, who always guides rightly, who gives the best advice—that friend is hidden in one's own heart. One cannot find a better one. Who is this friend? Man's own being, his true inner being. That friend is the origin, source, and goal of all.

But the question arises: if that friend is one's own being, why then call him a friend, why not call him one's self? The answer is that no doubt this friend is really one's own being, but when the greater Self is compared with the present realization, one finds oneself smaller than a drop in the ocean. Man cannot very well call that friend himself until he has forgotten himself, until he is no more himself. Until and unless one has arrived at the state of perfection, one had better be quiet and not insolent, talking about that which one has not yet become.

All occult schools all over the world prescribe as the first lesson quietude, no discussion, no dispute, no argument. The conditions for those on the path are altogether different from the conditions of the outer world. The true knowers of life have kept their lips closed on this subject. No method has been successful and profitable other than the method of the prophets of all lands, who gave man the first lesson of love for God.

Religious authorities of different times have kept humanity ignorant of the knowledge of God and have only given it a belief in God; and it is lack of this knowledge that has made the man of reason rebel against that which he could not understand. There remained no link between knowledge and belief, and that is how the reign of materialism came to the world—a reign that is still spreading. At such times of materialism chaos comes into the world; all is confusion and unrest. Many wish to do good, but do not know how. Such times Sri Krishna has called "the decay of dharma," when the spirit is gone and only the form remains. No doubt at times a warning comes to the soul in the form of intuition, but the intoxication of life, the mist, is so great that the message is not heard, not understood, not received, until the messenger has disappeared.

What is the manner and the method of the journey? We

see that when a person rises above all the things of the world, such as power, wealth, possessions, all that gives pride and vanity, there comes a desire in his heart—a remembrance of his origin, of the perfection of love and peace —although no one in the world can pretend to have arrived at this stage. Every moment of a man's life speaks louder of what he says than of what he really is.

Man's first tendency toward humanity is a loving, charitable attitude, to the extent that forgiveness dictates every action of his life. He shows patience in his actions, tolerance toward his fellowmen, and considers that each one has his own stage of evolution. He does not expect a person to act in a better way than his stage of evolution permits. He does not make his own law, wanting others to follow it; he follows the law for all.

When a man's attitude has become a loving attitude, and when he has developed a tendency to serve, to forgive, to tolerate, to have reverence for all, good and bad, young and old, then he begins his journey. To explain what path this is, there is no better symbol than the cross. No one without courage, strength of will, and patience can follow this path. When a person has to live among people of every different kind, he must make his own character soft as a rose, make it even finer, so that no one can be hurt by the thorns. Two thorns cannot harm each other. The thorns can hurt the rose, but the rose cannot tear the thorns. Think what the life of the rose between two thorns must be!

The journey begins with a path of thorns, and the traveler must go barefoot. It is not easy always to be tolerant and patient, to refrain from judging others, and to love one's enemy. It is a dead man who walks on this path, one who has drunk the bowl of poison. The beginning of each path is always difficult and uninteresting, hard for everybody. Ask the violinist about the first days when he practices scales and cannot even form the tones! Often he does not have enough patience to go on until he can play well enough to satisfy himself. The first part of the path is constant strife and struggle with life, but as one approaches the goal the path gets easier; the distance seems greater, but the path is smoother and the difficulties less. The journey is achieved by realizing in oneself the answer to the questions, "What am I? Am I body, mind, or what else? Do I originate from the earth or, if not, from where?"

As soon as one has started on the journey, one's lower nature rises up, and all one's follies and weaknesses want to drag one down to earth, and the struggle of breaking these chains requires the strength of a Samson. Then comes the struggle between the beauty of matter and spiritual beauty. Beauty in form and color is more realistic; spiritual beauty is hidden in mist until one comes to a stage when spiritual beauty becomes *the* beauty, which is a shining light.

When man has acquired knowledge, power, and magnetism, he becomes conscious of having greater power than others, of knowing more than others, and of being able to achieve more than others. To use these faculties rightly is another struggle. He should not pride himself on these accomplishments. There is an enemy who starts with him on the journey and never leaves him: his pride and spiritual egotism—and this enemy stays with him as long as he is on the path.

It is a great temptation to think, on having received inspiration and power, "I can do, know, understand more than you." It is a constant struggle until the end, and at any moment one may stumble and fall down. Only the steadfast traveller will persist in rising up every time, for without patience he may lose his way. But those who journey on this path will get help; as Christ said, "Seek ye first the kingdom of God, and all these things will be added unto you." It is the goal that is important, and so is the right attitude of the soul towards it, not the things one meets on the path.

Chapter 16.

THE PURPOSE FOR WHICH WE WERE BORN

When the spark that is to be found in every heart, the spark that may be called the divine spark in man, is blown upon and the flame arises, the whole of life becomes illuminated, and man hears and sees and knows, and understands.

When one inquires deeply into life, one finds that what all souls seek is to know the meaning of life. The scientist looks and searches for it in the realm of science, and the artist finds it in his art. Whatever different interests people may have, their only real inclination is to find the meaning of life. This shows that it is the nature of the soul and that the soul has come here for this purpose, that it may realize and understand the meaning of life. Thus, in either a material or a spiritual way, every soul is striving for what it longs for all the time, each in its own particular way.

One can see this in the behavior of an infant. The desire of an infant to look at a thing, to tear it to pieces and see what is inside it, shows that it is the soul's desire to look into life, to understand life. No doubt the effect and the influence of life on earth are intoxicating, and through this intoxication man becomes so absorbed in himself and his own interests that he so to speak loses the way—the way that is inborn in him. Not only in man, but even in the lower creation one finds the same attitude. In animals, in birds, the deepest desire is not looking for food or seeking a comfortable nest; the deepest tendency is the wish to understand the nature of life; and this tendency culminates in man. A child will continually ask his parents, "What does this mean?" and this shows a constant longing to know the meaning of life, a longing that continues all through life.

What does this teach us? It teaches us the principle that the source and goal of the universe are one and the same, and that the Creator created it all in order to know His own creation. But how does the Creator see and understand His creation? Not only in its highest and deepest aspect, but also through every thing and every being He is continually knowing and understanding His creation. For instance, if a person should ask, "What is art? Is it not made by man?" I would answer, "Yes, but made by God also, through man." And if that is so, then what is this whole mechanism of the universe doing? It is working. Working for what purpose? Working for the understanding of itself.

And what is this mechanism of the world; is it living or is it dead? All that we call living is living, and all that we call dead is living, too. It is for our convenience that we say "thing" and "being." In reality there are no things; they are all beings. There is simply a gradual awakening from the witnessing aspect to the recognizing aspect. And no science, however material, will deny the truth of this, for the truth is to be realized from all things—from religion, from philosophy, from science, from art, from industry. The only difference is that one takes a shorter way and the other takes a longer way; one goes around and about and the other takes a straight path. There is no difference in the destination; the only difference is in the journey—whether one goes on foot or whether one drives, whether one is awake or whether one is asleep and is taken blindly to the destination, not knowing the beauties of the way.

Destiny may be divided into two parts: one is the mechanism that activates the destiny, and the other is the soul that realizes this. Therefore, the mechanism is the machine and the soul within it is the engineer, who is there to work this mechanism and to produce by it what is to be produced. There are many methods and ways that man adopts in order to know and understand; and the mind is the vehicle, the tool, by the help of which he experiences life in the accomplishment of this purpose. In Sanskrit the mind is called *mana,* from which the English word *man* is derived; and that means that man is his mind, not his body.

According to the readiness of its tool, the soul experiences and knows life. It is the condition of the mind that enables the soul to see life clearly. The mind can be likened to water; when the water is troubled, there is no reflection to be seen; when the water is clear, then it shows the reflection. But in the pursuit of material gain, which is what he values most, man has become absorbed in that kind of life and has lost the benefit of life; as it is said in the Bible, "Where your treasure is, there will your heart be also."

When, as at the present time, one defines civilization as commercial or industrial progress, then that becomes the ideal of every soul; and it becomes difficult for a soul to retain tranquility in order to accomplish that purpose for which the soul was born. I do not mean by this that industrial or commercial development is not necessary for the life of man; not at all, as long as it does not ruin or hinder the purpose of life for which man was born. Otherwise, in spite of all his progress he will have wasted his life, and he will not have attained the purpose for which he was born.

There are superstitions in the East, and also in the West, that animals such as horses, dogs, cats, and birds, give warning when a person is about to fall ill or die, and many have found that there is some truth in these superstitions. Why is it, then, that man does not understand and perceive life as the animals do? The answer is that the animals live a more natural life; they are nearer to nature than man, who is absorbed in his artificial life.

So many of the things one thinks about and does and says are far from what is true, from what is natural. The more one can be at one with nature and at one with the deeper life, the more one realizes that what man does is to act continually against reality, not only when he does wrong or evil, but even when he is doing good. If the animals can know this, man is even more capable of knowing it; and it is this knowledge alone that is the satisfaction of his life, not all the external things; as it is said in the Bible. "The spirit quickeneth, the flesh profiteth nothing."

Where is man's wealth? It is in his knowledge. If his wealth is only in the bank and not in his knowledge, he does not really possess it; it is in the bank. All desirable and great things, values and titles, position and possession, where are they? Outside? No, because outside is only that which one knows by the knowledge one has within; therefore, the real possession is not without, but within. It is the self within, it is the heart that must be developed, the heart that must be in its natural rhythm and at its proper pitch. When it is tuned to its natural rhythm and pitch, then it can accomplish the purpose for which it is made.

There are five different ways by which the knowledge of life is perceived. One way is known to many of us, although to woman perhaps more than to man, and that is impression. Very often we come into a house, or we meet a person, and before we have spoken to that person we get a kind of impression, either pleasant or unpleasant—a certain knowledge of that person's being. Sometimes at the sight of a person we feel like saying, "Keep away"; sometimes at the first glance we feel drawn to a person without knowing the reason. The mind does not know, but the soul does. It is not only that one gets an impression of a person one meets, but if one is sensitive to impressions, one can also feel the impression of a letter that comes to one from a stranger. Many say that they can tell someone's character by physiognomy or phrenology, but if they do not have the sense of impression in their heart, then even if they were to read a thousand books on physiognomy or phrenology they would never get the true impression. What does this show? It shows that true knowledge, from beginning to end, does not belong to the material realm.

There is another way, and that is the intuitive way, by which one knows before one does something whether it will be a success or a failure. The more intuitive people feel this before doing or undertaking anything.

But then there is a third way, and that is the dream or the vision. Some will say that dreams have a meaning, while others hold that there is no meaning in a dream. But in point of fact, there is nothing in this world that has no meaning; there is no situation, no action, no word that has not its meaning. All that is done with intention and all that is done without intention has a meaning behind it, if one can only understand it.

The reason why one should see more clearly in a dream than when awake is that when a person is in a dream, his mind is naturally concentrated, for when man is in his waking state, all that is perceived through his senses calls his attention at every moment. No doubt the impression or intuition of a true dream is not manifested to every soul, and it is manifested to one soul more than to another; neither does everyone live always in the rhythm in which he can receive impressions and intuitions. At different times his impression differs, and in accordance with his evolution he is able to experience the knowledge of life. The more evolved he is spiritually, the more naturally he receives the knowledge of life from within.

The fourth way in which one can receive the knowledge of life is by what may be called inspiration. Inspiration may come to an artist, to a musician or to a poet, and at the time when it comes he can write or compose or do something that he will afterwards be surprised at, and he will wonder if he really did it himself or if it was done by someone else. If it had not been for inspiration, that same poet might have striven for months on end and not have been able to write the verse that he then wrote in a few minutes. What is the explanation of this? Is it by the development of his mind that a man receives inspiration? No, it is by the receiving quality of his mind, by the purity of his mind, his absorption in his art, the direction to which he has devoted his life. One might ask what would be the best way for an artist to receive inspiration: by waiting, by praying, or by continuing to work until inspiration comes? He should do all three together: wait for inspiration while working, and pray to God while waiting.

Where have the great souls whose inspirational works have become immortal gotten these works from? They have gotten them from inspiration. And how did they get this? They got it by forgetting themselves, by being absorbed in the object of their love. That is the meaning of sacrifice, sacrificing to the beauty of the ideal. One has to place the ideal before one, that is the way to get inspiration.

Souls get inspiration from outer life or from another person; in all names and forms there is a source of inspiration, if one only knew how to tap it. In point of fact, whether inspiration is received from outside or from within, it all comes from God. The only difference is that when it comes from within it is more direct; but the first step is to receive it from the outside.

All those who begin to receive inspiration receive it first from outer life. Man is created in such a way that he first looks outward; and then, when he is disappointed, when he cannot find all he wants in the outer life, he turns within. He wants to see if he can find it in the inner life, and thus he becomes connected with the source of inspiration that is the Spirit of guidance. And he who has once found the Spirit of guidance will always be able to find it again if he keeps close to it; but when he goes astray, when the way of his life takes another direction, then he wanders away from the Spirit of Guidance.

With still another step further, there comes the realization that may be called revelation. When the soul is tuned to that state, then the eyes and the ears of the heart are open to see and hear the word that comes from all sides. In point of fact, every atom of this world, either in heaven or earth, speaks, and speaks aloud. It is the deaf ears of the heart and the closed eyes of the soul that prevent man from seeing and hearing it. There is a verse of a Hindustani poet that says, "O self, it is not the fault of the divine Beloved that you do not see Him, that you do not hear Him. He is continually before you and He is continually speaking to you. If you do not hear it and if you do not see it, it is your own fault."

It is for this purpose that every soul has been created and it is in the fulfillment of this that man fulfills the object of God. When the spark that is to be found in every heart, the spark that may be called the divine spark in man, is blown upon and the flame arises, the whole life becomes illuminated, and man hears and sees and knows, and understands. A Sufi poet says that every leaf of the tree becomes like a page of the sacred book when the heart is open to read it and when the soul has opened its eyes.

Chapter 17.

THERE IS ONE VITAL SUBSTANCE

*Once the eyes of the heart are open, man begins to read
every leaf of the tree as a page of the sacred book.*

When we look at life and at the process of its development,
either from a mystical or from a scientific point of view, we
shall find that it is one life developing itself through different phases. In other words, there is one vital substance—call
it energy, intelligence, force, or light, call it God or spirit—
that is forcing its way through the most dense aspects of
nature, and that leads to its finest aspects. For instance, by
studying the mineral kingdom we find that there is a life in
it that is forcing its way out. We see that from the mineral
kingdom come substances such as gold and silver and precious stones. This means that there is a process by which
matter becomes finer and finer until it begins to show that
the spirit is of such radiance, intelligence, and beauty that
it even manifests through precious stones.

This is the scientific point of view; but when one adopts
a mystical point of view, then, if one is among rocks, if one
stands still in the mountains, if one goes alone into the

solitude, one begins to feel an upliftment, a sense of peace, a kind of at-one-ment with the rocks, hills, and mountains. What does this mean? It means that the same spirit that is in us is also in the mountain and rocks; it is buried in the rocks, as, in a lesser degree it is buried in ourselves, but it is the same spirit. That is why we are attracted to mountains, although mountains are not as living as we are. It is we who are attracted, not they. Besides, what can we give to the mountains? Restlessness, discord, our lack of harmony, our limitations. What can the mountains give us? Harmony, peace, calmness, a sense of patience, endurance. They inspire us with the idea that they have been waiting for perhaps thousands of years for an upliftment that comes through the development of nature from rock to plant, from plant to animal, from animal to man. This gradual unfoldment of the spirit is buried in all these different aspects of nature; and at each step, from rock to plant, from plant to animal, and from animal to man, the spirit is able to express itself more freely and is able to move more freely.

In this way, the spirit finds itself in the end; this shows that there is one purpose working through the whole of creation. The rocks are working out the same destiny as man, the plants are growing towards the same goal as man. What is that goal? Unfoldment. The spirit is buried in them and wants to make its way out. At each step of evolution there is a new unfoldment, a greater opening. From the animal, Darwin says, man has come. It might have seemed at the time that this was a new scientific discovery, but it was not so. A Persian poet, who lived seven hundred years before Darwin, says in poetic terms and in a religious form that God slept in the rock, dreamed in the plant, awoke in the animal, and realized Himself in man. And fifteen hundred years ago the Prophet Mohammad said the same in the Qur'an: that first was the rock, and afterwards the animals, and from them man was created.

The mystic sees a development of material life from rock to plant, from plant to animal, and from animal to the human physical body. This is one aspect, but only one. There is something else also, and that is the divine Spirit, the Light, the Intelligence, the All-consciousness. The one makes the earth, the other heaven. It is this Sun, this divine Spirit, that shines and projects its rays, each ray becoming a soul. Thus it is not true to say that man has developed from a monkey, and it is degrading the finest specimen of nature that God has created to call it an improvement of matter. That is a materialistic, limited conception. The soul comes directly from the divine Spirit. It is intelligence itself, it is the consciousness; but not the consciousness we know, for we never experience the pure existence of our consciousness. What we know of our consciousness is what we are conscious of, and therefore we only know what consciousness is in name.

There is no difference between pure intelligence and consciousness. We call pure intelligence consciousness when that intelligence is conscious of something, yet what we are conscious of is something that is before us. We are not that. We are the being who is conscious, not that of which we are conscious. The mistake is that we identify ourselves with what we see, because we do not see ourselves. Therefore man naturally calls his body himself, because he does not know himself. As he cannot find himself, what he identifies himself with is his body. In reality man is not his body, man is his soul. The body is something man possesses; it is his tool, his instrument with which he experiences life, but the body is not himself. Since he identifies himself with his body, he naturally says, "I live," "I die," "I am happy," "I am unhappy," "I have fallen," or " I have risen." Every condition of his limited and changeable body makes him think, " I am this." In this way he loses the consciousness of the ever-changing aspect of his own being.

The soul is the ray that, in order to experience life, brings with it an instrument, vehicles, and those vehicles are the body and the mind. Therefore, instead of "spirit, " we could just as well say the soul with its two vehicles, body and mind. Through the body it experiences outer conditions, and through the mind it experiences inner conditions of life. The soul experiences two spheres, the physical and the mental sphere; the mental sphere through the mind, and the physical sphere through the body and the five senses.

When we come to the evolution of the world according to the point of view of the mystic, we shall see that it is not that man has come from the plant and animal and rock, but that man has taken his body, his physical instrument, from the rock, from the animal and from the plant, whereas he himself has come direct from the spirit and is directly joined to the spirit. He is and always will be above that physical instrument that he has borrowed from the earth. In other words, man is not the product of the earth, but the inhabitant of the heavens. It is only his body that he has borrowed from the earth. Because he has forgotten his origin—the origin of his soul— he has taken the earth for his origin but the earth is only the origin of his body and not of his soul.

There is the question of what is the soul's natural unfoldment towards spiritual attainment. Spirituality apart, at every stage in one's life—infancy, the time from infancy to childhood, from childhood to youth, from youth to middle-age—at every further step there is a new consciousness. Childhood is quite a new consciousness compared with infancy. Youth is quite a different consciousness compared with childhood. In that way every soul, no matter what stage of life it is in and whether it knows it or not, has gone through many different unfoldments, each of which has given it a new consciousness. And there are experiences such as failure in business, or misfortune, or an illness, or some blow in life—it may be an affair of the heart or of money or a social matter; there are many blows that fall upon a person—and then a shell breaks and a new consciousness is produced. Very few will see it as an unfoldment, very few will interpret it as such, but it is so. Have we not all known among our acquaintances someone very uninteresting or with a disagreeable nature to whom we were never attracted, who then perhaps after a blow, a deep sorrow, or some other experience, awakens to a new consciousness and suddenly attracts us because he has gone through some kind of process?

Spiritual unfoldment is the ultimate goal of all mankind, and it comes at the moment when a person begins to be more thoughtful. When he begins to remember or to realize this yearning of the soul, consciously or unconsciously, a feeling comes—"Is this all I have to do in life, to earn money, to have high rank or position? If this is all, it is all a game. I have become tired of this game, I must think of something else. There is something else I have to attain." This is the beginning; this is the first step on the spiritual path. As soon as a person has taken this first step, his outlook is changed, his sense of values becomes different, and things to which he had attached great importance become of less importance; things that occupied him a great deal, he no longer concerns himself with. A kind of indifference comes over him. Nevertheless, a thoughtful person keeps to his duty just the same; in fact, he is more conscientious. There is greater harmony because he also begins to pity others.

And when he goes another step forward, there comes bewilderment. He begins to wonder, "What is it all for? Much ado about nothing!" I once saw in India a sage whom I knew to be very deep, a man of high attainment, and he was laughing at nothing. I wondered what he was laughing at. Then I stood there and looked around, thinking I must see from his point of view what was making him laugh so much. And I saw people hustling and bustling. For what? Was it not laughable? Every person thinking his particular point of view to be the most important! He pushes others away because he finds his action the most important. Is this not the picture of life? It is the way of the evolved and the unevolved. And what do they reach? Nothing. Empty-handed they leave this world; they have come without anything and they leave without anything.

It is this outlook that bewilders the soul. The sage does not feel proud when he laughs at others, although at the same time he finds it highly amusing; but he is just as amused at himself as at others.

And again, another step forward brings a person to an understanding that changes his outlook and manner. Generally, what happens is this: from morning until evening man reacts against everything, both good and bad. But good he sees very rarely; he always sees bad things. Or he meets someone who is nervous or excited or domineering or selfish, and so he experiences a jarring effect from everyone he meets. Then, without knowing it, his constant reaction will be one of despising, of hating, or of wishing to get away. This will be his continual feeling; and if he gets into the habit of saying, "I don't like, " "I dislike," he will soon be saying it from morning until evening with everyone he meets. This reaction he then expresses in word, thought, feeling, or action.

When one reaches this third stage of understanding, one begins to understand instead of reacting. Then there is no reaction, for understanding comes and suppresses it. It is just like the anchoring of a boat; it produces tranquillity, stillness, and weight in the personality. One no longer sways with every wind that blows; but one stays on the water like a heavy ship, not like a small boat that moves with every wave that passes. This is the stability one reaches in the third stage of unfoldment; and then one is ready to tolerate and to understand both the wise and the foolish.

It is a fact that the foolish person disagrees more with others than does the wise. One would think that he knew more than the wise! But the wise man agrees with both the foolish and the wise; the wise man is ready to understand everybody's point of view. He has his own ideas, his own way of looking at things, but he is capable of looking at things from the point of view of others, too. One eye alone does not see fully; to make the vision complete, two eyes are needed. So the wise can see from two points of view, and if we do not keep our own thoughts and preconceived ideas in check, if we cannot be passive, and if we do not wish to see from the point of view of other people, we make a great mistake. This third stage produces a tendency to understand every person one meets.

Then there is a fourth stage of the unfoldment. In that fourth stage one not only understands, but one sympathizes; one cannot but sympathize, for then one realizes that life in the world is nothing but limitation. Whether a person is rich, in a high position or in wretched circumstances, whatever condition he is in or whatever he is, he has to experience his limitation. This in itself is a great misery, and therefore every person has his problems. And when one begins to see that every person on this earth has a certain problem or burden he has to carry through life, one cannot but sympathize. The one who is awake to the pain of mankind, whether it is of his friend or his foe, cannot help but sympathize with him. Then he develops a tendency to reach out; he will always wish to reach out to every person he meets. And naturally by his sympathy he looks for good points, for if one looks at a person without sympathy one will always touch his worst points.

And when one goes a step further still, then the way is open to communicate. Just as there is a communication between two people who love each other, so the sympathy of a person who has achieved his soul's unfoldment is so awakened that not only every person, but even every object begins to reveal its nature, its character, and its secret. To him every man is an open book. We hear stories of saints and sages who talked with rocks and plants and trees. They are not just stories; this is a reality.

All the teachings given by the great prophets and teachers are only interpretations of what they have seen, and they have interpreted in their own language what they have read from this manuscript of nature; what trees, plants, and rocks said to them. Did they only speak with these in the past? No, the soul of man is always capable of that bliss, if he only realized it. Once the eyes of the heart are open, man begins to read every leaf of the tree as a page of the sacred book.

Chapter 18.

FOR THE ROSEBUD TO BLOOM

Is there even one soul, however materialistic, that does not wish to unfold? There cannot be.

It is in the unfoldment of the soul that the purpose of life is fulfilled. And this is true not only of human beings, but also of the lower creation, and even of objects of every kind; the fulfillment of their existence lies in their unfoldment. The clouds gather, and the purpose of this is shown when it starts raining. It is the unfoldment of that gathering of clouds that shows itself in rain; that purpose was not accomplished in the gathering of the clouds, which was only a preparation. One sees the same thing in nature, which works the whole year round, and in the appropriate season brings forth its fruits. Not only human beings, but even the birds and animals watch and delight in seeing the purpose of nature's continual activity being fulfilled in the spring.

We learn from this that every being and every object is working towards that unfoldment that is the fulfillment of its purpose. As Sa'di has said, "Every being is intended to be on earth for a certain purpose, and the light of that purpose has been kindled in his heart."

But behind all the different purposes that we see working through each individual, there seems to be one purpose, and that is the unfoldment of the soul. Knowing this, the ancient Hindus held this ideal before them in all walks of life. Not only those who sought after truth were seeking the soul's unfoldment, but an artist, a scientist, a learned person, a man of industry, or of commerce—each one believed that through his particular occupation he would be able to reach that goal. The great misfortune today is that people are so segregated in their different occupations that they have lost the thread that binds humanity into one, and gives that impetus from which all derive benefit. When the scientists stand on their ground strongly and firmly and the artists are absorbed in their sphere, the industrial workers in their world, and the people of commerce in the world of commerce, it is natural that their souls do not come in contact with one another, giving them a combined force for the betterment of the whole.

Although a degeneration caused by extreme materialism prevails throughout the whole world, it is not yet too late to find examples of personalities in all walks of life who still wish to arrive at the proper goal. Rabindranath Tagore translated into English a book of verse by Kabir, an uneducated man, a weaver from childhood whose livelihood depended upon his weaving; but through his continual seeking after unfoldment, he arrived at the goal. He told his experience in everyday language, but his book is looked upon by the people today as holy scripture.

This makes us wonder whether it is possible for scientists to arrive through their scientific studies, or artists through their art, or people of commerce through their trade, at that central truth that concerns every soul. When we look at humanity, we find that we can not only divide it into different races and different nations; we can also divide it into people of different occupations. In this age of materialism, the only thing that unites us is our material interest; but how long can we be united by a material interest? A friendship formed in materialism is not a friendship that will endure, nor can such friends depend upon each other. It is sacrifice that enables us to be friends and to co-operate with one another, and in sacrifice the sign of spirituality is seen; but we do not unite together in sacrifice today; our unity is in what we can gain in one way or the other. It is a matter for distress that in order to unite, we are holding fast to a lower ideal that will never prove a center of unity. It is only the high ideal that can unite, and in which we can hope to be united.

How can one define the unfoldment of the soul? The soul can be likened to the rose; as a rosebud blooms, so the soul unfolds itself. For the rosebud to bloom, five conditions are required: fertile soil, bright sun, water, air, and space; and the same five things are required for the unfoldment of the soul. As a fertile soil is required by the rosebush in order to grow, so education in the spiritual ideal should be given to the child from the moment it is born. When a child is deprived of that most important education in its childhood, then the soil is taken away from the roots of the rose. I can recall having met so many people who had every possibility and tendency to become interested in all that is spiritual and lofty, but who at the same time were afraid of the terminology in which it is expressed. What does this show? It shows that in childhood something was denied them, and now that they have grown up, although they feel a desire for it and although they want it, when they look at it in a form they are not accustomed to they are afraid of it.

Is there even one soul, however materialistic, that does not wish to unfold? There cannot be. Every soul has been born to unfold itself; it is its innate tendency, it cannot help it. But if the soul is deprived of the right condition, then it ceases to develop. Very often I have met people who did not believe in any particular religion, did not profess any particular faith, or adhere to any outward form, but in whom I have seen great spiritual qualities nevertheless.

The water that nourishes the rose is the love element. If that element is absent from anyone's life, however great his intellectual knowledge and his desire to seek after truth, he will still remain backward. Unfortunately, this element often seems to be missing in cultural life. A learned man will say that it has no place in the world of reason, and thus he separates the outer learning from the religious ideal that is called the love of God.

What is it that takes the part of the sun in the life of man, as the sun takes part in the growing of the rose? It is intelligence. Everyone may not seem to be intelligent, but the soul itself is intelligence. When the intelligence is covered by the mist of impressions, of ideas of this earth, that intelligence becomes drowned in something, buried under something. When it is discovered, then it is as bright as the sun. The mission of Buddha was mainly intended for this purpose. All that Buddha wished to teach his disciples was to discover that pure intelligence that is above all reasoning and is the essence of all reason.

The place that air occupies in the growth of the soul is this: air is symbolical of the inspiration that comes to the heart that is prepared for it. And it is not by outward learning but by what one learns through inspiration that the soul is raised towards its unfoldment.

The space that is needed around the rosebush in order to let it grow means symbolically a wide outlook on life. A person may live a hundred years, but with a narrow outlook he will never see the light. In order to see life clearly, the outlook should be wide. There is much to fight with in life in order to keep our outlook wide, for the nature of our life in the world is such that it drags us down and places us in conditions where we cannot but be narrow. A great person is not great because of his merits, his qualities or reputation; the surest proof that a person can give of his greatness is his vast outlook. And it is wonderful to notice how, even unconsciously, people who have arrived at that stage, in whatever walk of life, automatically begin to show a vast outlook on life. What fertilizes this plant and makes roses bloom is, symbolically, the teaching given by the great masters of humanity.

How can one recognize this development of the soul in which the purpose of life is fulfilled? What are its indications, its signs? The soul becomes like a rose, and begins to show the rose quality. Just as the rose consists of many petals held together, so the person who attains to the unfoldment of the soul begins to show many different qualities. These qualities emit fragrance in the form of a spiritual personality. The rose has a beautiful structure, and the personality that proves the unfoldment of the soul also has a fine structure: in manner, in dealing with others, in speech, in action. The atmosphere of the spiritual being pervades the air like the perfume of the rose.

The rose has seeds in its heart, and so the developed souls have in their heart that seed of development that produces many roses. The rose blooms and fades away, but the essence that is taken from the rose lives and keeps the fragrance that the rose had in its full bloom. Personalities who touch that plane of consciousness may live for a limited time on the earth, but the essence that is left by them will live for thousands and thousands of years, always keeping the same fragrance and giving the same pleasure that the rose once gave.

Chapter 19.

A LIGHT THAT WILL ALWAYS SHINE

*All the tragedy of life, all the misery and disharmony
are caused by lack of understanding, and lack of understanding comes from lack of penetration.*

There is a process of awakening from childhood to youth,
and from youth to maturity; and during this development
one's point of view, one's outlook on life, is changing. One
finds, too, that sometimes one goes through an illness or
great suffering, and at the end of it one's whole outlook on
life has changed. It also sometimes happens that someone
who has travelled far returns apparently quite altered.
Again, there often comes a sudden change of outlook after
a person has formed a friendship, or has been somebody's
pupil, or has married. There are even some cases where the
change is so marked that one can say he has become an
entirely new person.

We can divide such changes or developments into three
classes, of which the first is connected with the physical
development, the next with the development of the mind,

and the third with the development of the soul. Though few will admit it, many people can recollect experiences in their childhood when in one moment their whole outlook on life changed. Ripening is a desirable result, and it is the aim of every object in life to ripen and to develop; therefore in the awakening of the soul one may recognize the fulfillment of life's purpose.

The first sign of the soul's awakening is just like the birth of an infant. From the time of its birth the infant is interested in hearing things, whatever sound may come, and in seeing things, a color or light or whatever it may be; and thus a person whose soul has awakened becomes awake to everything he sees and hears. Compared with that person, everyone else seems to have open eyes and yet not to see, to have open ears and yet not to hear. Though there are many with open ears, yet there is rarely one who hears, and though there are many with open eyes, yet there is hardly one who sees. That is why the natural seeing of the awakened soul is called clairvoyance and its natural hearing clairaudience. The simple English word "seer" conveys that such a man has eyes, but as well as eyes he has sight.

The moment the soul has awakened, music makes an appeal to it, poetry touches it, words move it, art has an influence upon it. It no longer is a sleeping soul; it is awake and it begins to enjoy life to a fuller extent. It is this awakening of the soul that is mentioned in the Bible: unless the soul is born again, it will not enter the kingdom of heaven. For the soul to be born again means that it is awakened after having come on earth; and entering the kingdom of heaven means entering this world in which we are now standing, the same kingdom that turns into heaven as soon as the point of view has changed. Is it not interesting and most wonderful to think that the same earth that we walk on is earth to one person and heaven to another? And it is still more interesting to notice that it is we who change it from earth to heaven. This change comes not by study nor by anything else but the changing of our point of view. I have known people who seek after truth, study books about it, even write many books about philosophy and theology themselves, and in the end they were standing in the same place as before. That shows that all outer efforts are excuses; there is only one thing that brings one face to face with reality, and that is the awakening of the soul.

All the tragedy of life, all the misery and disharmony, are caused by lack of understanding; and lack of understanding comes from lack of penetration. When one does not look at life from the point of view that one should, then one is disappointed because one cannot understand. It is not for the outer world to help us to understound it better, it is we ourselves who should help ourselves.

Then there is a further awakening, a continuation of what I have called the awakening of the soul. And the sign of this awakening is that the awakened person throws a light, the light of his soul, upon every creature and every object, and sees that object, person, or condition in this light. It is his own soul that becomes a torch in his hand; it is his own light that illuminates his path. It is just like directing a searchlight into dark corners that one could not see before, and the corners become clear and illuminated; it is like throwing light upon problems that one did not understand before, like seeing through people with x-rays when they were a riddle before.

As soon as life becomes clear to the awakened soul, it shows another phase of manifestation, and this is that every aspect of life communicates with this person. Life is communicative, the soul is communicative, but they do not communicate until the soul is awakened. Once a soul is awakened, it begins to communicate with life. As a young man, I had a great desire to visit the shrines of saints and of great teachers, but although I wanted very much to hear something from them and to ask them something, I always held back my questions and sat quietly in their presence. I had a greater satisfaction in that way, and I felt a greater blessing by sitting quietly there, than if I had discussed and argued and talked with them, for in the end I felt that there was a communication that was far more satisfactory than these outer discussions and arguments of people who do not know what they discuss. It was enlightening and refreshing, and it gave the power and inspiration with which one can see life in a better light.

Those who are awakened become guiding lights not only for themselves but also for others. And by their light, often unknowingly, their presence itself helps to make the most difficult problems easy. This makes us realize the fact that man is light, as the scriptures have said, a light whose origin, whose source, is divine. And when this light is kindled, then life becomes quite different. Furthermore, when the soul is awakened, it is as if that person were to wake up in the middle of the night among hundreds and thousands of people who are fast asleep. He is sitting or standing among them, he is looking at them, hearing about their sorrows and miseries and their conditions, hundreds of them moving about in their sleep, in their own dream, not awakened to his condition, although he is near them. They may be friends or relations, acquaintances or enemies, but whatever may be their relationship, they know little about him, each one is absorbed in his own trouble. This awakened soul, standing among them all, will listen to everyone, will see everyone, will recognize all that they think and feel; but his language no one understands, his thoughts he cannot explain to anyone, his feelings he cannot expect anyone to feel. He feels lonely; but no doubt in this loneliness there is also the sense of perfection, for perfection is always lonely.

When it was said that upon the descent of the Holy Ghost the apostles knew all languages, it did not mean knowing the languages of all countries. I knew a man in Russia who spoke thirty-six languages, but that did not make him spiritual. The apostles, however, knew the language of the soul; for there are many languages that are spoken in different lands, but there are also numberless languages that are spoken by each individual as his own particular language.

And that helps us to realize another idea of very great importance: that the outer language can only convey outward things and feelings, but that there is an inner language, a language that can be understood by souls that are awakened. It is a universal language, a language of vibrations, a language of feeling, a language that touches the innermost sense. Heat and cold are different sensations, which are called by different names in different countries, and yet they are always essentially the same sensations. Also love and hate, kindness and unkindness, harmony and disharmony, all these ideas are called by different names in different countries, but the feeling is the same with everyone.

When, in order to know the thought of another person, we depend upon his outer word, we probably fail to understand it, for perhaps we do not know that person's language; but if we can communicate with another person soul to soul, we can certainly understand what he means, for before he says one word he has said it within himself; and that inner word reaches us before it is expressed outwardly.

Before the word is spoken the expression says it; before the thought has formed, the feeling speaks of it. And this shows that a feeling forms a thought, a thought that manifests as speech; and even before a feeling manifests it can be caught when one is able to communicate with the soul. This is what may be called communication: to communicate with the innermost being of a person. But who can communicate thus? The one who knows how to communicate with himself, the one who, in other words, is awakened. The personality of an awakened soul becomes different from every other personality. It becomes more magnetic, for it is the living person who has magnetism; a corpse has no magnetism. It is the living who bring joy, and therefore it is the awakened soul who is joyous.

And never for one moment think, as many do, that a spiritual person is a sorrowful, dried up, long-faced person. Spirit is joy, spirit is life; and when that spirit has awakened, all the joy and pleasure that exist are there. As the sun takes away all darkness, so spiritual light removes all worries, anxieties, and doubts. If a spiritual awakening were not so precious, then what would be the use of seeking it in life? A treasure that nobody can take away from us, a light that will always shine and will never be extinguished - that is spiritual awakening, and it is the fulfillment of life's purpose. Certainly, the things a person once valued and considered important become less important; they lose their value, and those that are beautiful lose their color. It is just like seeing the stage in daylight: all the palaces and other scenery on the stage suddenly mean nothing. But it puts an end to the slavery to which everyone is subjected, for the awakened man becomes master of the things of this world; he need not give them up. Optimism develops naturally, but an optimism with open eyes; power increases naturally, the power of accomplishing things, and he will go on with something until it is accomplished, however small it is.

It is very difficult to judge an awakened soul, as they say in the East, for there is nothing outwardly to prove its condition. The best way of seeing an awakened soul is to wake up oneself, but no one in the world can pretend to be awake when he is still asleep, just as a little child, by drawing a mustache on its face, cannot prove itself to be grown-up. All other pretences one can make, but not the one of being an awakened soul, for it is a living light. Truth is born in the awakening of the soul; and truth is not taught, truth is discovered. The knowledge of truth cannot be compared with the knowledge of forms or ideas; truth is beyond forms and ideas. What is it? It is itself and it is our self.

Very often people make an effort, though in vain, to awaken a friend or a near relation whom they love. But in the first place, we do not know if that person is more awakened than we ourselves; we may be trying for nothing. And the other point is that it is possible that a person who is asleep needs that sleep. Waking him in that case would be a sin instead of a virtue. We are only allowed to give our hand to the one who is turning over in his sleep, who desires to wake up; only then a hand is given. It is this giving of the hand that is called initiation. No doubt a teacher who is acquainted with this path may give a hand outwardly to the one who wishes to journey, but inwardly there is the Teacher who has always given and always gives a hand to awakening souls, the same hand that has received the sages and masters of all time in a higher initiation. Verily, the seeker will find sooner or later, if only he keeps steadily on the path until he arrives at his destination.

Chapter 20.

AND HE WILL NO MORE FIND HIMSELF TO BE WHAT HE THOUGHT HIMSELF TO BE

Life begins to reveal itself, and the whole of life becomes communicative.

The words "awake" and "asleep" are very familiar to us, as we use them in expressing different states in life. But in reality, when we look at it from the point of view of the soul, we are asleep and awake at the same time. For instance, when we are looking at a certain thing, when our mind is fully absorbed in it, we do not hear anything at that time. And when we are listening to something and are absorbed in what we are hearing, when our sense of hearing is thus focused, though our eyes may be open yet we are not seeing. This shows that when one sense is fully awakened the other senses are asleep. In the same way, the mind is absent while we are experiencing a sensation through the body; and when we have a sensation we are experiencing something through the mind, while the body takes no part in it. The more we look at sleeping and waking from the psychological point of view, the more we will find that they are not what we commonly understand by these words, but that every moment of the day and night we are both awake and asleep at the same time. Also, when a person is asleep and experiencing a dream, he is awake to something and yet asleep to the outer things. To one world he is asleep; to the other awake.

According to the mystics there are five stages of consciousness. One stage is our experience through the senses. In this condition our eyes are ready to see, our ears to hear; and we are awake to the outer world. This is the only aspect of wakefulness that we recognize as such, but there are four other aspects besides this one. The second aspect occurs when a person is asleep and yet is experiencing life exactly as he does on this plane of the physical world. This is the dream state; we call it a dream when we have woken up and have passed that stage. At the time of dreaming, that state is as real as this state in the physical world, and nothing is lacking in the dream that we find here. While dreaming we never think that it is a dream, but many things that we cannot find here on the physical plane we can find in the dream state. All the limitations and all that we lack in this life are provided for in the dream state. All that we are fond of, all that we would like to be, and all that we need in our life are easier to find in a dream than in the wakeful state. When we wake up and return to this life, we call it real and the other a dream, and we say that it was imagination, without any reality; we think that only on this physical plane are we awake, that only this is real. But is yesterday as real as today? Everything that has happened from the moment we came to earth, all that is past, is all yesterday; only just now is today. If it is not a dream, then what is it? We only recognize that which we saw in the dream as being just a dream; but all that is past is in reality nothing but a dream. It is "just now" that gives us the feeling of reality, and it is that which we are experiencing that becomes real to us, whereas that which we are not experiencing, of which we are not conscious, does not exist for us at this moment.

Thus everyone has his own life and his own world. His world is that of which he is conscious; and in this way everyone has his heaven and his hell, made by himself. We live in the world to which we are awakened, and to the world to which we are not awakened we are asleep. We are asleep to that part of life that we do not know.

Another experience is that of the man who lives in the world of music, whose thoughts and imaginings are about the composition of music, who enjoys it, to whom music is a language. He lives under the same sun as everybody else, and yet his world is different. Beethoven, who could no longer hear music with his ears, enjoyed the music he read and played, while perhaps another man with excellent hearing did not hear it. Beethoven's soul was in it, and the music was in himself.

Thus there is the kind of experience we have through our senses, our five senses; but this is one world, one plane of existence, and there is the other existence that we experience in the dream, and that is a world too, a different world with different laws. Those who consider the dream only as a dream do not know the importance, the greatness, the wonder of it. The dream plane is more wonderful than the physical plane, because the physical plane is crude, limited, and poor, and is subject to death and disease; the other plane, which one experiences in the dream, is better, purer, and one has a greater freedom there.

The third stage of consciousness is situated between spirit and matter. It is this that we experience as sleep, that condition that one calls deep sleep, when one does not even dream. There is so little said about it, and very few think about it. Once a person studies this question of sleep he will find that it is the greatest marvel in the world. It is a living phenomenon. The rest and peace, vitality and vigor, intelligence and life that come to man during the time of sleep are beyond explanation. And yet man is so ungrateful, he is never thankful for this experience, which is given to him every day; he is only unhappy when he has lost it. Then nothing in the world can satisfy him, no wealth, no comfort, no home, no position, nothing in the world can replace that experience that is as simple as sleeping, which means nothing and yet is everything.

The further we study the phenomenon of deep sleep, the more we will come to understand the mystery of life. It gives a key to the mystery of life, for it is an experience that divides our spiritual consciousness between the physical and spiritual worlds. It stands as a barrier between two experiences, one in this world, and one that is reached by spiritual attainment. The great Persian poet Rumi has written about sleep; he says, "O sleep! It is thou who makest the king unaware of his kingdom and the suffering patient forget his illness, and prisoners are free when they are asleep." All pains and sorrows and limitations of life, all the tragedy of life, all sufferings and agitations are washed away when one experiences that deep sleep.

It is a great pity that the mechanical and artificial life we live in this world today is depriving us of that natural experience of deep sleep. Our first fault is that we congregate and live in one city all crowded together. Besides, there are motorcars, trains, and tramways, and houses of twenty stories shaking every moment of the day and night. Every vehicle is shaking; and we are a race at the present time that is unaware of the comfort, the bliss, and the peace known to the ancient ones who lived simply with nature, far from our mechanical and artificial life. We are so far removed from the old ways that it has become our habit. We do not know any other comfort except the comfort we can experience in the kind of life we live; but at the same time, this shows that the soul is capable of attaining to greater comfort, pleasure, and joy, and to greater peace, rest, and bliss only by living naturally.

These three stages of conciousness—physical, dream, and deep sleep—are each nothing but an experience of the soul in an awakened state; but when a person is awake outwardly he is asleep to the inner world, and when he is fast asleep he is awakened to that particular plane and asleep both to dreamland and to the physical state.

When we have been looking at a bright light, and then that bright light is shut off, we see darkness. In reality there is no darkness, it only seems so; if there had not been a bright light before there would not be darkness but some light, for it is the contrast that makes it seem dark. Thus the experience that we have in our deep sleep is an experience of a higher and greater kind, and yet it is so fine, so subtle and unusual, because our consciousness is so accustomed to the rigid experiences of the physical world, and when we are in that other state the experience is too fine to perceive and to bring back to the physical world.

Every experience can be made intelligible by contrast. If there were no straight line we we could not say high and low, or right and left. It is the straight line that makes us recognize them as such. If there were no sun we could not say south, north, east, or west. Therefore, with every conception there must be some object to focus upon and with which to check our conception. With regard to deep sleep, we have nothing in physical existence to compare it to, and therefore the experience of deep sleep remains only as a great satisfaction, joy, and upliftment, and as something that has vitalized us and created energy and enthusiasm. This shows that there is something we have received from it. We do not come back empty-handed from there; we have gained something we cannot obtain from the physical plane. We get something we cannot interpret in everyday language, more precious, more valuable and vital than anything from the physical and mental planes.

There is a still higher plane or experience of consciousness, different from these three experiences, which everybody knows more or less; and this fourth experience is that of the mystic. It is an experience of seeing without the help of the eyes, hearing without the help of the ears, and experiencing a plane without the help of the physical body, in a way similar to that of the physical body but at the same time independent of it. And as soon as one arrives at this experience one begins to believe in the hereafter, for it gives one the conviction that when the physical body is discarded the soul still remains; that it is independent of the physical body and is capable of seeing, living, and experiencing, and of doing so more freely and fully. Therefore this stage of experience is called the consciousness of the mystic.

People become frightened when they hear about nirvana or mukti. Nirvana means to become nothing, and everyone wants to become something; no one wants to be nothing. There are hundreds and thousands interested in eastern philosophy, but when it comes to being nothing they find it a difficult thing to grasp, and they consider it most frightening to think that one day they will be nothing. But they do not know that it is the solving of this question that makes a person into a being, because what he believes himself to be is a mortal thing that will one day expire, and he will no more find himself to be what he thought himself to be.

Nirvana, therefore, is the fifth consciousness. It is a consciousness similar to that of a person in deep sleep. But in deep sleep one is asleep outwardly, that is to say in the physical body, while the mental body is also asleep. In this condition of nirvana or highest consciousness, however, one is conscious all through of the body as much as of the soul. During this experience a person lives fully, as the consciousness is evenly divided, and yet he remains conscious of the highest stage.

To conclude, what does the soul's awakening mean? The body's awakening means to feel sensation; the mind's awakening means to think and to feel; the soul's awakening means that the soul becomes conscious of itself. Normally man is conscious of his affairs, of the conditions of life, of his body and mind, but not of his soul. In order to become conscious of the soul one has to work in a certain way, because the soul has become unconscious of itself. By working through its vehicles, body and mind, it has become unaware of its own freedom, of its own beauty.

The first stage in the awakening of the soul is a feeling of dissatisfaction with all that one knows, with all the knowledge one may have, whether of science, art, philosophy, or literature. A person comes to a stage where he feels there is something else he must know that books, dogmas, and beliefs cannot teach, something higher and greater that words cannot explain. That is what he wants to know. It does not depend on age. It may be a child who has that inclination, or a man who may already have reached a considerable age. It depends upon the soul; therefore in the East they call a child an old soul when it begins to show that inclination, when it is not satisfied with the knowledge of names and forms.

Then there comes a second stage, and that stage is bewilderment. Imagine an evolved person being more bewildered than an unevolved one! And yet it is so, for at this stage a man begins to see that things are not as they seem to be but as they are. This causes a kind of conflict; he does not know whether to call a thing good or bad, love or hate. There comes a time when all that he had accepted in his mind, all that he believed in, now appears to be quite the contrary to what it seemed before: his friend, his relations, those whom he loved, everything; wealth, position, all the things he has pursued, all change their appearance and sometimes seem to become quite the opposite of what they were.

Once in Chicago a lady came to see me, trembling, in a very sorrowful state of mind. I asked her what was the matter. She said she had had an accident. The house in which she lived had been burnt down and she had had to break a window in order to get out. She had hurt her hand, and it had all upset her very much. But then she said, "It is not the fire that has upset me so." I asked, "What, then?" She said, "The way that all my friends and neighbors, whom I loved and liked, acted when the fire started has impressed me so that the whole world is quite different now." What does this mean? That friendship, relationship, love, or devotion may not be the same as they appeared when it comes to the time of test. There comes a time when our consciousness changes our outlook on life; and it changes as soon as our soul has opened its eyes. Then our whole life changes; we live in the same world and yet do not live in it; it becomes quite a different world.

And the next stage after this bewilderment is the stage of sympathy. We begin to appreciate things more and sympathize more, for up to now when we walked on thorns we did not feel them. But at this stage we begin to feel them, and seeing that others are walking on the same thorns we forget our pain and begin to sympathize with them. The evolved ones become sympathetic; they develop a natural tendency of outpouring. Troubles, sufferings, and limitations—everyone has to go through them, everyone has to face the same difficulties. And not only the good; the wicked have still greater difficulties. They live in the same world with their wickedness, they have a great load to carry. If one can see this, one naturally becomes forgiving and sympathetic.

And as one goes further in the soul's unfoldment, one finally arrives at the stage of revelation. Life begins to reveal itself, and the whole of life becomes communicative. The evolved soul will feel the vibrations of every other soul; and every condition, every soul, every object in the world will reveal its nature and character to him.

Chapter 21.

THE LIFTING OF THE VEIL

You yourself it is who have made yourself a captive, and it is you yourself who will try to make yourself free.

Day and night are not conditions of the sun; they are conditions in themselves. The sun neither rises nor sets. That is our conception: it is more convenient to speak of the rising of the sun and the setting of the sun. If anything rises and sets, it is the world, not the sun. When the world turns its back to the sun, it is night; when the world turns its face to the sun, it is day.

It is the same with the soul's awakening. The soul is always awake. But what is it awake to? Someone may be looking with open eyes; but what is he looking at? Is he looking upward or downward or sideways? A person is only conscious of the direction in which he is looking.

To speak of the soul's awakening, therefore, is for the sake of convenience. What part of us is it that may be called "soul"? As it is not our body, then what is it? It is something that is beyond the body and beyond the mind. It is conscious, and at the same time its consciousness is not as we understand it, for the word "consciousness" conveys that one is conscious of something. Though not everyone knows what consciousness means, everyone knows what he is conscious of. For instance, a mirror in which something is reflected is not only a mirror, it is a mirror with a reflection, which means it is occupied; it is not empty. When a person speaks of consciousness he cannot think of the original condition; he can think only of the consciousness that is conscious of something. As soon as we distinguish between the consciousness and what it is conscious of, we separate them, as we separate the mirror from what is reflected in it.

When one has realized this, one will come to the conclusion that the soul of the wise and of the foolish, of the sinner and of the virtuous, is one and the same. The wickedness of the wicked and the goodness of the good, the ignorance of the foolish and the wisdom of the wise, are apart from the soul: the soul is conscious of it. When another person is conscious of it, he may say that here is a wise or an ignorant soul. But the soul is the same; it is not the soul that is ignorant or wise, wicked or virtuous, but what is reflected in it. At the same time, one should know that if an elephant is looking into a mirror, the mirror is not the elephant, but one can see an elephant in the mirror. But if a man does not know what a mirror is, he will say that here is an elephant, although it is only its relfection; it is nothing but a mirror when it is free from this reflection. The moment the reflection is removed, the mirror will again be just a mirror.

And so it is with the soul. Man makes it miserable, wicked, ignorant, wise, or illuminated by being conscious of these things. The soul is neither the one nor the other. The soul is only soul. This misconception creates great difficulties.

If the soul is conscious, what is it then? The best explanation one can give is that it is the essence of all things; it is life. But not life in the sense we understand it; that is only a suggestion of life. The soul is the real life. We say of one who moves and sees and hears and acts that he is a living being, but what is living in him is the soul. The soul is not seen, and therefore life is not seen. Life has touched a person, and therefore on seeing the effect of that touch one says, "He is living, it is life." But what we see is only a suggestion of life, which appears and disappears. Life is living and never dies.

We have the same problem with intelligence as with consciousness. One knows intelligence as something that is intelligent; but there is a difference between intelligence and something that is intelligent. Intelligence in which a certain consciousness is reflected becomes intelligent, but intelligence need not know, in the same way that consciousness need not be conscious of anything; it is the knowing faculty. If one keeps a person in a dark room with striking colors and beautiful pictures, he cannot see them. His eyes are open, his sight is all right, but what is before him is not reflected in his sight. What is there is sight, but nothing is reflected in it. So it is with consciousness, and so it is with intelligence; intelligence, which is consciousness, and consciousness, which is the soul.

Science today says that there is a gradual awakening of matter towards consciousness and that matter becomes fully intelligent in man. The mystic does not deny this; but where does matter come from? What is it? Matter is intelligence just the same. It is only a process, so if intelligence manifests in man it is the development of matter. But intelligence that is intelligent begins with intelligence and culminates in intelligence. Spirit is the source and soul of all things. If matter did not have spirit in it, it would not awaken, it would not develop. In matter life unfolds, discovers, realizes the consciousness that has been, so to speak, buried in it for thousands of years. By a gradual process it is realized through the vegetable and animal kingdoms and unfolds itself in man, and then resumes its original condition. The only difference is that in this completion, this fulfillment of the spirit that manifests in man, there is variety. There is such a large

number of beings, millions and billions, but their origin is
only one Being; therefore spirit is one when unmanifested,
and many in the realm of manifestation; the appearance of
this world is variety. The first impression man gets is that
of many lives, and this produces what we call illusion, which
keeps man ignorant of the human being. The root from
whence he comes, the original state of his being, man does
not know. He is all the time under the illusion of the world
of variety, which keeps him absorbed and interested and
busy, and at the same time ignorant of his real condition, for
just as long as he is asleep to one side of life and awakened
to the other, asleep to the inner and awakened to the outer.

One may ask how one awakens to this inner life, what
makes one awaken, and whether it is necessary for one to
be awakened. The answer is that the whole of creation was
made in order to awaken. But this awakening is chiefly of
two kinds: one kind is called birth, the birth of the body
when the soul awakens in a condition where it is limited, in
the physical sphere, in the physical body, and by this man
becomes captive. And there is another awakening, which is
to awaken to reality, and that is called the birth of the soul.
The one awakening is to the world of illusion, the other to
the world of reality.

But one must know that there is a time for everything, and
when one does not pay heed to this one makes a mistake.
When one wakes a person at two o'clock in the morning his
sleep is broken; he ought to sleep all night, he needs this.
Very often people, not knowing this, try to wake someone
up, it may be their wife, their husband, their friend, their
relation, or their child. Someone may feel very anxious to
awaken another. Often he feels lonely and thinks, "He is
close to me; he should be awake too." It is the same with the
one who smokes or drinks: he likes someone else to do it
with him, just as it is dull for a person in a cheerful mood
if another person cannot see the joke. Naturally, therefore,
the desire and tendency of the one who awakens to the
higher life, to reality, is to awaken others. He cannot help

it; it is natural. If it were not, he would say, "Well, I experience it, I enjoy it; is that not enough? Why must I trouble about others who stand in front of me like stone walls?" Such people have toiled their whole life and they have been exiled and flayed and martyred and crucified, and when they have awakened to a certain sphere where they enjoy harmony and peace they wish that others too may experience it and enjoy it in the same way. But very often we are too impatient and unreasonable, and want to awaken people before it is time.

The other day I was touched to see a play* in which a student of the light, of the higher ideals, pronounces the word, the sacred word, and dies. And the remarkable thing was that there was a sage in the play who saw it and said, "He saw beyond and died."

What does death mean? Turning. The soul is always awake and therefore it is always living, but it may turn from one side to the other side. If there is some beautiful voice coming from behind to which it wishes to listen, then it turns towards it; and in the same way, when it is attracted to a certain sphere to which it had been asleep before, that is called awakening.

We see that the time for nature to awaken is the spring. It is asleep all winter and it awakens in the spring. And there is a time for the sea to awaken; when the wind blows and brings good tidings as if to awaken it from sleep, then the waves rise. All this shows struggle, shows that something has touched the soul that makes it uneasy, restless, that makes it want liberation, release. Every atom, every object, every condition, and every living being has a time of awakening. Sometimes this is a gradual awakening and sometimes it is sudden. To some people it comes in a moment's time by some blow or disappointment, or because their heart has broken through something that happened suddenly. It may have appeared cruel, but at the same time the result was

---

*Hazrat Inayat Khan refers to Ansky's play *The Dybbuk*.

a sudden awakening, and this awakening brought a blessing beyond words. The outlook changed, the insight deepened; joy, quiet, indifference, and freedom were felt, and compassion showed in the attitude. A person who would never forgive, who liked to take revenge, who was easily displeased, who would measure and weigh everything, when his soul is awakened, becomes in one moment a different person. As Mahmud Ghasnavi, the emperor poet of India, has said in most beautiful words, "I, the emperor, have thousands of slaves awaiting my command, but the moment love had sprung in my heart I considered myself the slave of my servants."

The whole attitude changes. Only, the question is what one awakens to, in which sphere, in what plane, to which reality. Sometimes, after one has made a mistake, by the loss that mistake has caused the outlook becomes different. In business, in one's profession, in wordly life, a certain experience, just like a blow, has broken something in someone; and with that breaking a light has come, a new life. But it is not right to awaken someone by mistake. No doubt very often awakening comes by a blow, by great pain; but at the same time it is not necessary to look for a blow. Life has enough blows in store for us; we need not look for them.

In order to get a clear idea of awakening, one should consider the condition that we call dreaming. Many attach little importance to it. If somebody says, "That person is dreamy," he means to say that he is not conscious of anything. But is there in reality anything that we can call a dream? The real meaning of dream is that which is past. Yesterday is as much a dream as the experience of the night: it is past. When a person is dreaming, does he think that he is in a dream, does he think that it is unimportant, does he give it any less importance than his everyday life at that moment? He looks at it as a dream when he has awakened to this other sphere, although in that sphere he will not call it a dream. If a person were asked when he is dreaming, "what about the experience of yesterday?" He would say,

"It was a dream"—"And what about everyday life?" "It was all a dream."

The more one thinks of it, the more one happens to glance into the hereafter, the more one will realize that what the hereafter is— what is behind the veil of death—is the awakening to another sphere, a sphere as real as this one or even more real. For what is real? It is the soul, the consciousness itself, that is real. What is past is a dream; what will come is hope. What one experiences seems real, but it is only a suggestion. The soul is real, and its aim is to realize itself; its liberation, its freedom, its harmony, its peace all depend upon its own unfoldment. No outer experience can make the soul realize the real.

Why cannot we see the soul as we can see the body? From our thought we can understand that we have a mind, because thought manifests to us in the form of a mental picture, but why do we not see the soul? The answer is that as the eyes cannot see themselves, so it is with the soul: it is sight itself, and therefore it sees all. The moment it closes its eyes to all it sees, its own light makes it manifest to its own view. It is for this reason that people take the path of meditation, the path by which they get in touch with themselves; they realize the independence and the continuity of life, which is immortal life, by getting in touch with their soul.

As to those who come into this world in a miserable condition, while others come in good conditions, this is not something in the soul. It is something the soul has carried along with it like the camel's load, which is on its back and not in the camel itself.

In spiritual awakening, the first thing that comes to man is a lifting of the veil, and that means the lifting of an apparent condition. Then a person no longer sees every condition as it appears to be, but behind every condition he sees its deeper meaning. Generally man has an opinion about everything that appears before him. He does not wait one moment to look patiently, he immediately forms an opinion about every person, every action he sees; whether it is wrong or right, he immediately forms an opinion without knowing what is beyond. It takes a long time for God to weigh and measure; but for man it takes no time to judge! When, however, the veil of immediate reason is lifted, then one reaches the cause, then one is not awakened to the surface but to what is behind the surface.

Then there comes another step in awakening. In this man does not even see the cause, but he comes to the realization of the adjustment of things; how every activity of life, whether it appears to be wrong or right, adjusts itself. By the time a person arrives at this condition he has lost much of his false self. That is what brings him there, for the more one is conscious of the false self, the further one is removed from reality; these two things cannot go together. It is dark or it is light; if it is light there is no darkness. The more the false conception of self is destroyed, the more light there is. It is for this reason that a person who is on the path sees life more clearly.

Another form of awakening is the awakening of the real self. Then one begins to see what one's thoughts and one's feelings mean, what right and wrong mean. Then man begins to weigh and measure all that springs up within himself. The further one goes, the more one sees behind things, the more one becomes attached to all planes of existence, not only living on the surface of life. This is a new kind of awakening; then a person has only to be awakened to the other world; he need not go there. He need not experience what death is, for he can bring about a condition where he rises above life. Then he comes to the conclusion that there are many worlds in one world; he closes his eyes to the dimensions of the outer world and finds within his own self, in his own heart, the center of all worlds. And the only thing that is necessary is turning; not awakening, but turning.

Man has become motionless, stagnant, by attaching himself to this world into which he is born and in which he has become interested. If he can make his soul more supple and thus be able to turn away from all this, he can experience all that has been said of the various planes of different worlds, which are in reality different planes of consciousness. Only by being able to make his soul supple, by making his soul able to turn, will he find the whole mystery within himself.

The Sufis distinguish fourteen planes of existence, which they call *choudatabaq*. It is a mystical conception: these planes are the expression of the fourteen different states of consciousness experienced by the help of meditation; the lowest of them is called *pata loka*. In the experience of these fourteen planes the djinn plane and the angelic plane are also touched.

We need not awaken ourselves to every particular plane; we should awaken to every plane as we go on in life's journey. What is necessary is to be wide awake in life and to see what is asked of us by our friend, by our neighbor, or by the stranger who is travelling with us; becoming more and more considerate, and observing what is expected of us; asking ourselves, "Do we harm him or do we serve him; are we kind to that person or do we hurt him?" For we try to get what we do not have in life, and in doing so we are often inclined to forget whom we push away and to whom we are unkind. The one who observes this rule reduces his mistakes from a thousand to a hundred; it does not mean that he will become faultless, but if he can avoid nine hundred mistakes out of a thousand, that is already something.

But no deed, however good it may appear, is a virtue unless it is willingly done, because in the willingness to do it, even in a sacrifice, one expresses the breath of freedom. A virtue forced upon ourselves or upon another is no virtue. It loses its beauty. We must do what we think is good.

A Sufi poet showed wherein lies the solution of this problem when he said, "You yourself it is who have made yourself a captive, and it is you yourself who will try to make yourself free."

Chapter 22.

THE INNER LIFE: THE CONSCIOUSNESS OF PERFECTION

Man is a phenomenom far greater than any other mechanism, if only he had the patience and perserverance to explore himself.

There is one aspect of life that is known to us, our everyday life in which we are conscious of all that we do, and this aspect may be called the outer life. There is another part of our life of which we are very often unconscious, and which may be called the inner life. To be without inner life is like being without an arm or a leg or an eye or an ear; but even that does not really illustrate the idea of the inner life. The reason is that the inner life is much greater and nobler and much more powerful than the outer life. Man gives great importance to the outer life, being absorbed in it from morning until evening and not being conscious of the other aspect. Thus all that matters to man is what happens to him in his outer life, and the occupations of his outer life keep him so absorbed that he has hardly a moment to think of the inner life.

The disadvantage of not being conscious of the inner life is incomparably greater than all the advantages one can gain by being conscious of the outer life, for the inner life makes one richer, the outer life poorer. With all the riches and treasures that the earth can offer man is poor; and very often the richer he seems the poorer he is, for the greater the riches, the more limitation he finds in his life. The inner life makes one powerful, whereas the consciousness of the outer life makes one weak, because it is the consciousness of limitation. The consciousness of the inner life makes one powerful because it is the consciousness of perfection. The outer life keeps one confused; however intellectual or learned a person may be, his mind will never be clear, for his knowledge is based upon reasons, which in turn are founded upon the outer things that are liable to change and destruction. That is why, however wise this person may seem to be, his wisdom has limitations.

The inner life makes the mind clear, for it is that part of one's being that may be called divine, the essence of life, the pure intelligence; and wherever the light of pure intelligence is thrown, things become clear. Absorption in the outer life, without that which the inner life can give, makes one blind; all that one says, thinks, or does is based upon outer experiences; and one cannot realize to what extent the power gained by the inner life enables one to see through life.

Inner life may also be called spiritual life. One can see it in the forest where it is the rain from above that makes the forest beautiful; this means that the forest alone does not have all that it needs, but that it needs something that comes from above: the light and the rain. It is the sun and the rain that make the forest complete. In the desert there is no rain, and therefore it is incomplete; there is the earth, but there is not water, nor is there water from above. The water that gives life to the forest is not to be found in the desert. The desert is unhappy, and the man in the desert is unhappy too, looking for shade from the hot sun; for the desert is longing, and the man in the desert is longing too for something he cannot find; whereas in the deep forest there is joy, there is inspiration, the heart is lifted up, because the forest is a picture of the inner life–not just the earth, not just the trees and plants—but because something it needs has been sent down to it. And so it is with man: a man who is solely occupied with the things of the world is in the midst of the world, but he is in the desert. It is the inner life that produces in him, not artificial virtues and man–made qualities, but those virtues that can only arise from the inner life, and also the insight that makes the eyes see more than mortal eyes can see.

That question is, how are we to be sure that there is an inner life, what proof is there? And the answer is that there is not one moment in our life when we do not see the proof of the inner life, only we do not look for it. All the different means of communication, such as telepathy and telephone and radio, all the new machines and inventions that make people marvel at what mankind has accomplished, are, if man would only realize it, nothing but a poor imitation of what this human body is! Man is the center of joy, of happiness, of peace, of power, of life, and of light. Man is a phenomenon far greater than any other mechanism, if only he had the patience and perseverance to explore himself. But what we do is to explore others. We think it is very important to analyze things, and the analysis of human nature we call psychology. Man analyzes everyone except himself, and therefore true psychology is never reached; because the real psychology is to analyze oneself first, and when one's self is analyzed, then one is able to analyze others.

If man only knew that besides what he says or does or thinks, and the effects that are manifest to him, there is another kind of action,which also creates things in a person's life, and which makes his world! And perhaps in a week or in a month, or perhaps in a year or ten years, that which he has thus created one day comes before him as a world, as a world created by him. Such is the phenomenon of life. How insignificant of a human being appears to be, just like a drop in the sea, yet what effects does he create by every thought, by every feeling, by every act! And what influence they spread, what influence they have on the lives of others! If one only realized this, one would find that the results of all one thinks, says, or does in the outer life are incomparably smaller than the results produced by what one thinks, says, or does in the inner life. Thus the consciousness of the inner life makes man more responsible than that of the outer life. The responsibilities of the outer life, compared with the responsibilities of the inner life, are much smaller. For the moment they might appear to be heavy burdens, but they are nothing compared with the responsibilities one has in one's inner life. If one sees what one creates, the responsibility becomes much greater. There is a saying in the East that the donkey seems to be much happier than the *chakor,* which is supposed to be the most intelligent bird. Man seems quite pleased in outer life, because his responsibilities are less, his outlook small, his horizon narrow, and what he sees of the world is very little; but when the horizon is opened up, when the heart has penetrated through the barrier that divides the here and the hereafter, when he begins to see behind the veil and all that appears on the surface becomes a screen behind which something else is hidden, then he experiences life quite differently.

The view of the one who stands on top of the mountain is quite different from the view of the one who stands at its foot. Both are human beings, both have the same eyes, but their horizons are different. Inner life, therefore, means the widening of the horizon and the change in direction of seeing. A mystic is often called a seer; and a great yogi has said, "In order to see what is before you, you must first see within yourself." This means that within oneself there is a mirror, and it is that mirror that may be called the inner world, the inner life. It is in this mirror that all that is before one is reflected. When the eyes are looking outward one turns one's back to the mirror, which is inside; but when the eyes are turned inward, then one sees reflected in this mirror all that is outside. By this process all seeing becomes so clear and manifests to such fullness that compared with it the outer vision is a blurred or confused vision.

Two persons may live together for twenty–five years, for forty or for fifty years, and may still not be able to understand one another because of the lack of inner life; yet the inner life would enable them to understand one another in a moment. When it is said that the twelve Apostles began to understand the language of all nations, does it mean that they learned the grammar of all nations at that moment? No, they learned the language of the heart. The language of the heart speaks more loudly than words can speak. If the ears of the heart were open to hear that language, outer words would not be necessary.

Humanity, in spite of all its progress, is still most limited; and the more one sees the limits of this progress, the more one finds that it is because of the absence of inner life. When one reads in stories and histories of the past how many thieves and robbers and highwaymen there used to be, and how many murders were committed, one feels that it was a dreadful time. And yet when one thinks more deeply about it one sees that the situation at present is much worse and that the days of robbers and highwaymen were much milder. Then one or two persons in a village were murdered; now towns and countries are swept away. War has swept away a large part of humanity. Imagine if another war comes —what will be the result? They say people have progressed, that they are more thoughtful, but with all this thoughtfulness they seem only to have progressed in order to cause destruction and disasters to a much greater degree. Does it mean that humanity is not progressing? It is progressing, but in which direction? Downward.

It is a condition of taking the path of the inner life that one should first be free. If the feet are pinned and the hands are nailed by beliefs, by preconceived ideas, by one's thoughts, then one stands still; one may have every desire to go on, but one is not going on, because one is holding on to something. When a person is holding on to certain beliefs, he is not going forward. And with many good qualities and high ideals, with religious tendencies, with a devotional temperament, with all the spiritual qualities that one may have, yet one can still remain standing in the same place. Either these ideas are holding the feet as if with nails, or the hands are somewhere holding on to the railing and not letting one go further.

What the inner life requires first is freedom to proceed. The old meaning of freedom is very little understood, although everyone is seeking freedom. So much is said about freedom, but one can be free of everything except one thing, and that is the self—the last thing one thinks about. The conception of freedom is quite different at this time, and although he is seeking freedom, man is anything but free, because he is caught in the trap of his own self. This is the greatest captivity there is; there he remains like the djinn in the bottle.

The inner life also requires sacrifice. Man considers that his learning, his qualifications, everything in his life, are there in order that he may gain everything he can in the world—power, possessions, wealth, anything—and believing that sacrifice is quite contrary to gain, he thus develops in himself a nature for gaining instead of sacrificing. Besides, sacrifice requires a large mind, it requires deep sympathies, great love; sacrifice is the most difficult thing. Inner life is something that in within oneself; it has been called a chamber of divine light in one's heart. The door remains closed until an effort is made to open it, and that effort is sacrifice. The Bible speaks of self-denial; but this is often misinterpreted. Self-denial, according to general belief, means denying oneself all that is good and beautiful, all that is worth attaining; but in reality self-denial does not mean denying oneself all that is good and beautiful, it means denying the self; and that is the last thing one wishes to deny. And the automatic action of this denial is to open the door to the inner life.

The sages who have realized the inner life have realized it by contemplative means. Man from his infancy is unaware of that something in him that is more than a faculty. By experiencing life only through the outer senses, this faculty, which is the faculty of inner life, becomes closed through not being used, and this is just as if the door of a chamber of joy and light and life were closed. And as from infancy one has not experienced the joy and life and light of this chamber, which may be called a celestial chamber in the heart of man, one remains unaware of it.

Nevertheless, one may sometimes have this feeling unconsciously; and sometimes when one is deeply touched, when one has suffered deeply, when life has shown its hideous side, or after an illness, or by the help of meditation, this feeling, which is unconsciously working as a longing to unfold itself, becomes manifest. In what way? In love of solitude, in sympathy for others, in a tendency towards sincerity, in the form of inspiration coming from all that is good and beautiful. It may manifest in the form of emotion, love, or affection, in the form of inspiration or of a revelation or a vision, or as art, poetry, or music; in whatever form one allows it to express itself, or with whatever one happens to be occupied, it begins to manifest in that form.

Everything becomes spiritual once this door of the chamber of the heart is open. If a man is a musician, then his music is celestial: if he is a poet, then his poetry is spiritual; if he is an artist, then his art is a spiritual work; whatever he may do in life, the divine spirit manifests. He need not be a religious person, he need not be philosopher, he need not be a mystic. It is simply that what was hidden in him and was thereby keeping his life incomplete begins to manifest to view, and that makes his life perfect; it enables a man to express life in its fullness. Every attempt made today to better the condition of humanity through politics, education, social reconstruction, and many other ways, all these, however excellently planned, can only be fulfilled if this something that was missing is added to them; but in the absence of this, all the efforts of many, many years will prove to be futile. For this something that is missing is the most essential of all. The world cannot remain a world without rainfall. The world cannot progress without a spiritual stimulus, a spiritual awakening. It need not be the first thing, it is natural that it should not be so; but it should at any rate be the last thing, and if it is not even the last, then it is most regrettable.

How are the mediative souls awakened, how do they experience the inner life? In the first place, the adept values his object of attaining the inner life more than anything else in life. As long as he does not really value it, so long he remains unable to attain it. That is the first condition: that man should value the inner life more than anything else in the world, more than wealth, power, position, rank, or anything else. It does not mean that in this world he should not pursue the things he needs; it means he should value most something that is really worthwhile.

The next thing is that when one begins to value something one thinks it is worthwhile giving time to it; for in the modern world it is said that time is money, and money today means the most valuable thing. So if a person gives his precious time to what he considers most worthwhile, more so than anything else in the world, then that is certainly the next step toward the inner life. And the third thing is that the condition of his mind should be relieved of that pressure that is always in a person's heart, when he thinks that he has not done what he ought to have done towards his fellow men, be it father, mother, child, husband, wife, brother, friend, or whoever it is.

If the pressure is troubling the mind, then that mind is not yet ready. A person may give his valuable time to contemplation, to a spiritual life, yet at the same time his mind is disturbed and his heart is not at rest, for he feels he has not done his duty, he has a debt to pay to someone. It is an essential point that the adept takes care that any debt to be paid in life does not remain unpaid. When we look at life, is it not a market place? The give and take is to be seen in everything, and if one does not pay now, the bill will be presented afterwards. And if one thinks that one has gained something without paying, in the end one will realize that one has to pay with added interest.

Man does not know in what form he has to pay, nor in what form he does the taking; very often he does not know when he takes or what he gives; but every moment of his life is occupied in give and take, and all the injustice of the world adjusts itself in the end. A clear understanding of this condition will show that it all balances. If there were no balance the world would not exist. This ever–moving world, turning round and round, what holds it, what makes it sta-ble? It is balance. And not only the world, but everything else, too: the whole of life in its own way. Being occupied by our worldly life, we are not aware of that balance, but when the inner eye is open and one sees life clearly, one will find that there is a continual balancing process going on. and that we as particles of one mechanism are constantly busy keeping this balance. When once the heart is at rest through the feeling that one has paid or is paying one's debts, then one comes to a balanced condition in life. Then the heart, which is likened to the sea, is no longer restless as it is during the storm. It becomes like calm, undisturbed water, and it is that condition that enables man to experience inner life more fully.

Do we not often notice the disturbing presence of people who have not got that tranquillity, that peace, that calm-ness? It is a terrible influence upon themselves and a disas-trous influence upon others. One can realize this in one's everyday life. One may be sitting in an office with someone, one may be standing in a certain place, one may be staying in a house where other people are, and one can realize by their atmosphere whether they have reached a state of balance, tranquillity, calm, and peace, or whether they are out of rhythm, unbalanced. This shows that what we call happiness and unhappiness is a question of a balanced or an unbalanced state. When a person's mind and heart are in the state in which they ought normally to be, he need not seek for happiness; he is happiness itself, he radiates happiness. When that state is disturbed he is unhappy; it is not that unhappiness comes to him, but that he himself is unhappiness.

The Hindu idea is that self means happiness, that the depth of the self is happiness. This means that all this outer structure, the physical body, the breath, the senses of perception, all of which help to make man, are most important; but his inner being can be called by only one name, and that is happiness. It is natural, therefore, that everyone should be seeking for happiness, though not knowing where to get it and always seeking for it outside himself; and instead of finding the happiness that is his own, he tries to get the happiness of another; but what happens is that he can neither get happiness from another, nor can he give it. By trying to get it from another, he causes sorrow to that one, and the sorrow comes back to him.

The robbers who go into other people's houses to steal are few in number, but there are many robbers of happiness, and they seldom know that they are robbing others of their happiness. The robber of happiness is more foolish than the robbers who go after wealth, for when the latter are successful they at least get something; but the robber of happiness never gets anything. He only gives sorrow to others.

Inner life, therefore, must not be considered, as many have thought it to be, a life that is spent in the forest or in a cave of the mountain or in retirement. Naturally, certain people need to seek solitude–those who prefer to be away from the turmoil of the world, whose inspiration is stimulated and who find themselves by being alone; but it is not a necessity for attaining happiness. One can be in the midst of the world and yet stand above the world. Life has many woes, and the only way to get rid of them is to stand above them all; and this can be attained by one thing and one thing only—the discovery of the inner life.

Chapter 23.

PREPARING FOR THE JOURNEY

There is no one living a settled life here; all are unsettled, all are on their way.

The inner life is a journey, and before setting out upon it there is a certain preparation necessary. If one is not prepared, there is always the risk of having to return before one has arrived at one's destination. When a person goes on a journey, and when he has to accomplish something, he must know what is necessary on the path and what he must take with him, in order that his journey may become easy and that he may accomplish what he has started to accomplish. The journey one takes in the inner life is as long as the distance between the beginning of life and death, it being the longest journey one ever takes throughout life; and one must have everything prepared, so that after reaching a certain distance one may not have to turn back.

The first thing that is necessary is to see that there is no debt to be paid. Every soul has a certain debt to pay in life; it may be to his mother or father, his brother or sister, to his husband or wife or friend, or to his children, his race, or to humanity; and if he has not paid what is due, then there are cords with which he is inwardly tied, and they pull him back. Life in the world is fair trade, if one could only understand it—if one knew how many souls there are in this world with whom one is connected or related in some way, or whom we meet freshly every day. To everyone there is something due; and if one has not paid one's obligations, the result is that afterwards one has to pay with interest.

There is the inner justice that is working beyond the worldly justice, and when man does not observe that inner law of justice, it is because at that time he is intoxicated, his eyes are closed, and he does not really know the law of life. But that intoxication will not last; there will come a day when the eyes of every soul will be opened; and it is a pity if the eyes open when it is too late. It is better that the eyes are opened while the purse is full, for it will be very difficult if the eyes open at the time when the purse is empty. To some consideration is due, to some respect, to some service, to some tolerance, to some forgiveness, to some help. In some way or other, in every relationship, in every connection there is something to pay; and one must know before starting the journey that one has paid it, and be sure that one has paid it in full, so there is nothing more to be paid. Besides this, it is necessary that man, before starting his journey, realizes that he has fulfilled his duties, his duty to those around him and his duty to God. But the one who considers his duty to those around him sacredly does his duty to God.

Man must also consider, before starting on his journey, whether he has learned all he desired to learn from this world. If there is anything he has not learned, he must finish it before starting the journey. For if he thinks, "I will start the journey, although I had the desire to learn something before starting, " in that case he will not be able to reach his goal; that desire to learn something will draw him back. Every desire, every ambition, every aspiration that he has in life must be gratified. Not only this, man must have no remorse of any kind when starting on his journey, and no repentance afterwards. If there is any repentance or remorse, it must be finished before starting. There must be no grudge against anybody, and no complaining of anyone having done him harm, for all these things that belong to this world, if man took them along, would become a burden on the spiritual path. The journey is difficult enough, and it becomes more difficult if there is a burden to be carried. If a person is lifting a burden of displeasure, dissatisfaction, or discomfort, it is difficult to bear it on that path. It is a path to freedom, and to start on this path to freedom man must free himself, no attachment should pull him back, no pleasure should lure him back.

Besides this preparation, one needs a vehicle, a vehicle in which one journeys. That vehicle has two wheels, and they are balance in all things. A man who is one-sided, however great his power of clairvoyance or clairaudience, whatever be his knowledge, still is limited; he cannot go very far, for it requires two wheels for the vehicle to run. There must be a balance, the balance of the head and the heart, the balance of power and wisdom, the balance of activity and repose. It is the balance that enables man to stand the strain of this journey and permits him to go forward, making his path easy. Never imagine for one moment that those who show lack of balance can ever proceed further on the spiritual journey, however greatly in appearance they may seem to be spiritually inclined. It is only the balanced ones who are capable of experiencing the external life as fully as the inner life; to enjoy thought as much as feeling; to rest as well as to act. The center of life is rhythm, and rhythm causes balance.

On this journey certain coins are necessary also, to spend on the way. And what are these coins? They are thoughtful expressions in word and in action. On this journey man must take provision to eat and drink, and that provision is life and light. And on this journey man has to take something in which to clothe himself against wind, and storm, and heat, and cold; and that garment is the vow of secrecy, the tendency to silence. On this journey man has to bid farewell to others when starting, and that farewell is loving detachment; before starting on this journey he has to leave something behind with his friends, and that is happy memories of the past.

We are all on the journey; life itself is a journey. No one is settled here; we are all passing onward, and therefore it is not true to say that if we are taking a spiritual journey we have to break our settled life; there is no one living a settled life here; all are unsettled, all are on their way. By taking the spiritual journey you are only taking another way, one that is easier, better, and more pleasant. Those who do not take this way, also will come in the end; the difference is in the way. One way is easier, smoother, better; the other way is full of difficulties; and as life has no end of difficulties from the time one has opened one's eyes on this earth, so one may just as well choose the smoother way to arrive at the destination at which all souls will sometime arrive.

By "inner life " is meant a life directed towards perfection, which may be called the perfection of love, harmony, and beauty; in the words of the orthodox, towards God.

The inner life is not necessarily in an opposite direction to the worldly life, but the inner life is a fuller life. The worldly life means the limitation of life; the inner life means a complete life. The ascetics who have taken a direction quite opposite to the worldly life have done so in order to have the facility to search into the depths of life; but going in one direction alone does not make a complete life. Therefore, the inner life means the fullness of life.

In brief, one may say that the inner life consists of two things: action with knowledge, and repose with passivity of mind. By accomplishing these two contrary motions, and by keeping balanced in these two directions, one comes to the fullness of life. A person who lives the inner life is as innocent as a child, even more innocent than a child; but at the same time wiser than many clever people put together. This shows as a development in two contrary directions. The innocence of Jesus has been known through the ages. In his every movement, in his every action, he appeared to be as a child. All the great saints and sages, the great ones who have liberated humanity, have been as innocent as children and at the same time wiser, much more so, than the worldly-wise. And what makes it so? What gives them this balance? It is repose with passiveness. When they stand before God, they stand with their heart as an empty cup; when they stand before God to learn, they unlearn all things that the world has taught them; when they stand before God, their ego, their self, their life, is no more before them. They do not think of themselves in that moment with any desire to be fulfilled, with any motive to be accomplished, with any expression of their own; but as empty cups, that God may fill their being, that they may lose the false self.

Therefore the same thing helps them in their everyday life to show a glimpse of the quiet moment of repose they had with God. They show in their everyday life innocence and yet not ignorance; they know things and they do not know. They know if somebody is telling a lie; but do they accuse that person? Do they say, "You are telling a lie"? They are above it. They know all the plays of the world, and they look at them all passively; they rise above the things of this world, which make no impression on them. They take people quite simply. Some may think that they are ignorant in their lives in the world, because they take no notice of things that are of no importance. Activity with wisdom makes them more wise, because it is not everybody in this world who directs his every action with wisdom. There are many who never consult wisdom in their action and there are others who seek refuge under wisdom after their action— and very often it is then too late. But the ones who live the inner life all direct their activity with wisdom; every moment, every action, every thought, every word is first thought out, is first weighed, and measured, and analyzed before it is expressed. Therefore, everything they do in the world they do with wisdom, but before God they stand with innocence; there they do not take worldly wisdom.

Man often makes mistakes, either by taking one way or the other, and therefore he lacks balance and does not come to touch perfection. For instance, when he takes the way of activity in the path of God, he also wishes to use his wisdom there; in the path of God he also wishes to be active, where he does not need action. It is just like swimming against the tide; where you must be innocent, if you use your wisdom there it is the greatest error. Then there are others who are accustomed to take passivity as a principle with which they stand before God in their innocence; and they wish to use the same principle in all directions of life, which would not be right.

Chapter 24.

TO MAKE GOD A REALITY

The work of the inner life is to make God a reality.

The first and principal thing in the inner life is to establish a relationship with God, making God the object to whom we relate ourselves, such as the Creator, Sustainer, Forgiver, Judge, Friend, Father, Mother, and Beloved. In every relationship, we must place God before us, and become conscious of that relationship so that it will no more remain an imagination; because the first thing a believer does is to imagine. He imagines that God is the Creator, and tries to believe that God is the Sustainer, and he makes an effort to think that God is a Friend, and an attempt to feel that he loves God. But if this imagination is to become a reality, then exactly as one feels for one's earthly beloved sympathy, love, and attachment, so one must feel the same for God. However greatly a person may be pious, good or righteous, yet without this his piety or his goodness is not a reality to him.

The work of the inner life is to make God a reality, so that He is no longer an imagination, so that this relationship man

158

has with God may seem to him more real than any other relationship in this world; and when this happens, then all relationships, however near and dear, become less binding. But at the same time, a person does not thus become cold; he becomes more loving. It is the godless man who is cold, impressed by the selfishness and lovelessness of this world, because he partakes of those conditions in which he lives. But the one who is in love with God, the one who has established his relationship with God, his love becomes living; he is no more cold; he fulfills his duties to those related to him in this world much more than does the godless man.

Now, as to the way in which man establishes this relationship, which is the most desirable relationship to establish with God, what should he imagine? God as Father, as Creator, as Judge, as Forgiver, as Friend, or as Beloved? The answer is that in every capacity of life we must give God the place that is demanded by the moment. When, crushed by the injustice, the coldness of the world, man looks at God, the perfection of justice, he is no longer agitated, his heart is no longer disturbed; he consoles himself with the justice of God. He places the just God before him, and by this he learns justice; the sense of justice awakens in his heart, and he sees things in quite a different light.

When man finds himself in this world motherless or fatherless, then he thinks that there is the mother and father in God; and that, even if he were in the presence of his mother and father, these are only related on the earth. The motherhood and fatherhood of God is the only real relationship. The mother and father of the earth only reflect a spark of that motherly and fatherly love that God has in fullness and perfection. Then man finds that God can forgive, as the parents can forgive the child who was in error; then man feels goodness, kindness, protection, support, sympathy coming from every side; he learns to feel that it comes from God, the Father-Mother, through all.

When man pictures God as Forgiver, he finds that there is not only a strict justice in this world, but that love is

developed also; there is mercy and compassion, there is that
sense of forgiveness—that God is not the servant of law, as
is the judge in this world. He is Master of law. He judges
when He judges; when He forgives He forgives. He has both
powers. He has the power to judge and He has the power
to forgive. He is Judge because He does not close His eyes
to anything man does; He knows, He weighs and measures,
and He returns what is due to man. And He is Forgiver,
because beyond and above His power of justice there is His
great power of love and compassion, which is His very being, which is His own nature, and therefore it is more, and
in greater proportion, and working with a greater activity
than His power of justice. We, the human beings in this
world, if there is a spark of goodness or kindness in our
hearts, avoid judging people. We prefer forgiving to judging.
Forgiving gives us naturally a greater happiness than taking
revenge, unless a man is on quite a different path.

The man who realizes God as a friend is never lonely in
the world, neither in this world nor in the hereafter. There
is always a friend, a friend in the crowd, a friend in the
solitude; or while he is asleep, unconscious of this outer
world, and when he is awake and conscious of it. In both
cases the friend is there in his thought, in his imagination,
in his heart, in his soul.

And the man who makes God his Beloved, what more
does he want? His heart becomes awakened to all the beauty
there is within and without. To him all things appeal, everything unfolds itself, and it is beauty to his eyes, because God
is all-pervading, in all names and all forms; therefore his
Beloved is never absent-because the whole tragedy of life is
the absence of the beloved. To one whose Beloved is always
there, when he has closed his eyes the Beloved is within,
when he has opened his eyes the Beloved is without. His
every sense perceives the Beloved; his eyes see Him, his ears
hear His voice. When a person arrives at this realization he,
so to speak, lives in the presence of God; then to him the
different forms and beliefs, faiths and communities do not

count. To him God is all-in-all; to him God is everywhere. If he goes to the Christian church, or to the synagogue, the Buddhist temple, the Hindu shrine, or the mosque of the Muslim, there is God. In the wilderness, in the forest, in the crowd, everywhere he sees God.

This shows that the inner life does not consist in closing the eyes and looking inward. The inner life is to look outwardly *and* inwardly, and to find one's Beloved everywhere. But God cannot be made a beloved unless the love element is awakened sufficiently. The one who hates his enemy and loves his friend cannot call God his Beloved, for he does not know God. When love comes to its fullness, then one looks at the friend with affection, on the enemy with forgiveness, on the stranger with sympathy. Love in all its aspects is expressed when love rises to its fullness; and it is the fullness of love that is worth offering to God. It is then that man recognizes in God his Beloved, his Ideal and by that, although he rises above the narrow affection of this world, he is the one who really knows how to love even his friend. It is the lover of God who knows love, when he rises to that stage of the fullness of love.

The whole imagery of the Sufi literature in the Persian language, written by great poets, such as Rumi, Hafiz, and Jami, is the relationship between man as the lover and God as the Beloved; and when one reads understanding that, and develops in that affection, then one sees what pictures the mystics have made and to what note their heart has been tuned. It is not easy to develop in the heart the love of God, because when one does not see or realize the object of love, one cannot love. God must become tangible in order that one may love Him, but once a person has attained to that love he has really entered the journey of the spiritual path.

Chapter 25.

THE ATTAINMENT OF THE INNER LIFE

By "inner life" is meant a life directed towards perfec-
tion, which may be called the perfection of love, har-
mony, and beauty; in the words of the orthodox,
towards God.

In the attainment of the inner life there are five things necessary. The first thing that is necessary is the mastery of mind;
and this is done by unlearning all that one has learned. The
inner knowledge is not gained by adding to the knowledge
one has already achieved in life, for it requires a rock foundation. One cannot build a house of rocks on a foundation
of sand. In order to make the foundation on rocks, one has
to dig into the sand and build the foundation on the rocks
below. Very often, therefore, it becomes difficult for an intellectual person, who through life has learned things and
understood them by the power of intellect, to attain to the
inner life. For these two paths are different: the one goes to
the north and the other goes to the south. When a person
says, "I have now walked so many miles to the south, shall

I therefore reach sooner something that exists in the north?" he must know that he will not reach it sooner, but later, because as many hours as he has walked to the south he must walk back in order to reach the north.

Therefore it must be understood that all man learns and experiences in this life in the world, all that he calls learning or knowledge, is only used in the world where he is learning, and bears the same relation to himself as the eggshell does to the chick; but when he takes the path to the inner life, that learning and knowledge are of no use to him. The more he is capable of forgetting that knowledge, of unlearning it, the more capable he is of attaining the object for which he treads the spiritual path. It has been a great struggle for those learned and experienced in the outer life to think that after their great advancement in worldly knowledge they have to go back again. Often they cannot understand; many among them think it is strange, and are therefore disappointed. It is like learning the language of a certain country, when one wants to go into another country where that language is not understood and whose language is not understood by oneself. Just as there is the north pole and the south pole, so there is the outward and the inward life. The difference is still vaster, because the gap between the inner life and the outer life is vaster than the distance between the north pole and south pole. The one who advances to the south is not getting nearer to the north pole, but, on the contrary, is going further from it; in order to reach it he must turn right around. However, it is not difficult for the soul that is an earnest traveller on the path. It is only a matter of using the enthusiasm in the opposite direction—to turn the enthusiasm one has for learning something of the world into forgetting and unlearning it, in order to learn something of the inner life.

Now the question is, how does one unlearn? Learning is forming a knot in the mind. Whatever one learns from experience or from a person, one makes a knot of it in the mind; and there are as many knots found as there are things one has learned. Unlearning is unravelling the knot; and it is as hard to unlearn as it is to untie a knot. How much effort it requires, how much patience it requires, to unravel when one has made a knot and pulled it tight from both sides! So it requires patience and effort to unravel the knots in the mind. And what helps the process? The light of reason working with full power unravels the mental knots. A knot is a limited reason. When one unravels it, its limitation is taken away; it is open. And when the mind becomes smooth by unlearning and by digging out all impressions, of good and bad, of right and wrong, then the ground of the heart becomes as cultivated ground, just as the land does after plowing. All the old stumps and roots and pebbles and rocks are taken off, and it is made into ground that is now ready for the sowing of the seed. But if there are rocks and stones and bricks still scattered there, and still some of the old roots lying there, then it is difficult for the seed to be sown; the ground is not in the condition the farmer wishes it to be.

The next thing in the attainment of the inner life is to seek a spiritual guide, someone whom a man can absolutely trust and have every confidence in; someone, he can look up to and with whom he is in sympathy, which would culminate in what is called devotion. And if once he has found some-one in life whom he considers his guru, his murshid, his guide, then he can give to him all confidence, so that not a thing is kept back. If there is something kept back, then what is given might just as well be taken away, because everything must be done fully: either have confidence or not have confidence, either have trust or no trust. On this path of perfection all things must be done fully.

Now there are the particular ways of the guide, which depend upon his temperament and upon his discrimination in finding for everyone who is being guided a special way. He may lead them to their destination by the royal road, or through the streets and lanes; down to the sea or through the town, by land or by water—the way that to him seems the best under certain circumstances.

The third thing necessary for spiritual attainment is the receiving of knowledge. This being the knowledge of the inner world, it cannot be compared with the knowledge one has learned before. That is why it is necessary to unlearn the latter. Man cannot adjust what he receives in this path to the ideas he has held before; the two things cannot go together. Therefore there are three stages of receiving knowledge that the one being guided has to go through. The first stage is that of receiving the knowledge, when he does nothing but receive. The next stage is the period after this, and that stage is that of assimilating what has been learned. Man thinks upon it, he ponders upon it, in order that it may remain in his mind. It is just like eating food and then assimilating it. The third stage is that of reasoning it out by oneself. Man does not reason it out as soon as he has received it; if he did, he would lose the whole thing, because it is like a person who has learned A and B and C at one stage, and then would ask how about words that did not begin with those letters. He would reason it out much sooner than he ought, for he has not yet learned the other letters. There is a time that must necessarily be given to receiving, as one gives time to eating. While one is eating one does not run about in the street in order to assimilate the food. After a person has finished his dinner, then he does everything possible to help digest it. Assimilating is clearly understanding, feeling and memorizing knowledge within oneself; not only that, but waiting until its benefit and its illumination come as a result of achievement.

The third part, then, to the receiving of knowledge is reasoning, to reason it through: why was it like that? What benefit has come to me from it? How can it be made practicable in life? How can it benefit myself and others? That is the third stage. If these stages are confused, then the whole process becomes confused, and one cannot get that benefit for which one treads the spiritual path.

The fourth grade of attainment of the inner life is meditation. If one has unlearned all that one has learned, if one has a teacher, and if one has received the knowledge of the inner life, still meditation is a thing that is most necessary, which in the Sufi term is called *ryazat.* In the first place, meditation is done mechanically, at an hour one has fixed upon as the hour for devotion or concentration. The next step is to think of that idea of meditation at other times during the day. And the third stage is continuing meditation throughout the day and night. Then one has attained to the right meditation. If a person does meditation only for fifteen minutes in the evening and then forgets altogether about it all day, he does the same thing as going to church on Sunday and then the other days of the week forgetting all about it.

Intellectual training no doubt has its use in the achievement of the inner life, but the principal thing is meditation. That is the real training. The study of one year and the meditation of one day are equal. By this meditation is meant the right kind of meditation. If a person closes his eyes and sits doing nothing, he may just as well go to sleep. Meditation is not only an exercise to be practised; in meditation the soul is charged with new light and life, with inspiration and vigor; in meditation there is every kind of blessing.

Some become tired of meditation, but that does not mean that they meditate; they become tired before having arrived at a stage where they really experience the effect of meditation, like those who become weary of practicing the violin. They are tired because they have not yet played the violin; if once they played, they would never be weary. The difficulty is in playing the violin, and the difficulty is having patience with one's own playing.

Patience is required in meditation; a person gets tired because he is accustomed to activity throughout the day. His nerves are all inclined to go on and on in that activity, which is not really for his benefit and yet is giving him the inclination to go on; and when he sits with his eyes closed he feels uncomfortable, for the mind which has been active all day becomes restive, just like a horse after having had a long run: then if you want that horse to stand still, it is restive. It cannot stand still, because every nerve has been active, and it becomes almost impossible to keep that horse still.

And so it is with man. Once I was with a man who was in the habit of meditating, and while we were sitting near the fire and talking about things he went into the silence, and I had to sit quiet until he opened his eyes. I asked him, "It is beautiful, is it not?" and he said, "It is never enough." Those who experience the joy of meditation, for them there is nothing in this world that is more interesting and enjoyable. They experience the inner peace and joy that cannot be explained in words; they touch perfection, or the spirit of light, of life and of love—all is there.

The fifth necessity in the spiritual path is that of loving the everyday life. There are no strict morals that a spiritual guide enforces upon a person, for that work has been given to the outward religions. It is to the exoteric side of spiritual work that the outer morals belong, but the essence of morals is practiced by those treading the spiritual path. Their first moral principle is constantly to avoid hurting the feeling of another. The second principle is to avoid allowing themselves to be affected by the constantly jarring influences that every soul has to meet in life. The third principle is to keep their balance under all different situations and conditions that upset this tranquil state of mind. The fourth principle is to love unceasingly all those who deserve love, and to give to the undeserving their forgiveness; and this is continually practiced by them. The fifth principle is detachment amidst the crowd; but by detachment I do not mean separation. By detachment is meant only rising above those bondages that bind man and keep him back from his journey towards the goal.

Chapter 26.

TO BECOME ALL THINGS TO ALL MEN

The inner life is a birth of the soul . . . and with this
new birth there comes the assurance of everlasting life.

The principle of the one who experiences the inner life is to become all things to all men throughout his life. In every situation, in every capacity, he answers the demand of the moment. Often people think that the spiritual person must be a man with sad looks, with a long face, with a serious expression, and with a melancholy atmosphere. Really speaking, that picture is the exact contrary of the real spiritual person. In all capacities the one who lives the inner life has to act outwardly as he ought in order to fit the occasion; he must act according to the circumstances, and he must speak to everyone in his own language, standing upon the same level, and yet realizing the inner life.

For the knower of truth, the one who has attained spiritual knowledge and who lives the inner life, there is no occupation in life that is too difficult; as a business man, a professional man, a king; as a ruler, a poor man, a worldly man; as a priest or monk, in all aspects he is different from what people know and see of him. To the one who lives the inner life the world is a stage; on this stage he is like the actor who has to act a part in which he has sometimes to be angry and sometimes loving, and in which he has to take part in both tragedy and comedy. So also the one who has realized the inner life acts constantly; and, like the actor who does not feel the emotions he assumes, the spiritual man has to fill fittingly the place in which life has placed him. There he performs everything thoroughly and rightly, in order to fulfill his outer commission in life. He is a friend to his friend, a relative to his relatives. With all to whom he is outwardly related he keeps the right relationship with thought and with consideration; and yet in his realization he is above all relationships. He is in the crowd and in the solitude at the same time. He may be very much amused, and at the same time he is very serious. He may seem very sad, and yet there is joy welling up from his heart.

Therefore the one who has realized the inner life is a mystery to everyone; no one can fathom the depth of that person, except that he promises sincerity, he emits love, he commands trust, he spreads goodness, and he gives an impression of God and the truth. For the man who has realized the inner life every act is his meditation; if he is walking in the street it is his meditation; if he is working as a carpenter, as a goldsmith or in any other trade or business, that is his meditation. It does not matter if he is looking at heaven or at the earth, he is looking at the object that he worships. East or west or north or south, upon all sides is his God. In form, in principle, nothing restricts him. He may know things and yet may not speak; for if a man who lives the inner life were to speak of his experiences it would confuse many minds.

There are individuals in the world who from morning until evening have their eyes and their ears focused on every dark corner, wanting to listen, or to see what they can find out; and they find out nothing. If someone were to tell such people wonders, he would have a very good occupation— the whole world would seek him. But such is not the work of the self-realized man. He sees, and yet does not look; if he were to look, how much he would see! There is so much to be seen by one whose every glance, wherever it is cast, breaks through every object and discovers its depth and its secret. And if he were to look at things and find out their secrets and depths, where would it end, and of what interest is it to him?

The inner life, therefore, is seeing all things and yet not seeing them; feeling all things and not expressing them, for they cannot be fully expressed; understanding all things and not explaining. How far can such a man explain, and how much can another understand? Each according to the capacity he has, and no more. The inner life is not lived by closing the eyes; one need not close one's eyes to this world in order to live it, one can just as well open them.

The exact meaning of the inner life is not only to live in the body, but to live in the heart, to live in the soul. Why, then, does not the average man live an inner life when he too has a heart and a soul? It is because he has a heart, and yet is not conscious of it; he has a soul, and knows not what it is. When he lives in the captivity of the body, limited by that body, he can feel a thing only by touching it, he sees only by looking through his eyes, he hears only by hearing with his ears. How much can the ears hear and the eyes see? All this experience obtained by the outer senses is limited. When man lives in this limitation he does not know that another part of his being exists that is much higher, more wonderful, more living, and more exalted. Once he begins to know this, then the body becomes his tool, for he lives in his heart. And then later he passes on and lives in his soul. He experiences life independently of his body; and that is called the inner life. Once man has experienced the inner life, the fear of death has expired, because he knows death comes to the body, not to his inner being. When once he begins to realize life in his heart and in his soul, then he looks upon his body as a coat. If the coat is old he puts it away and takes a new one, for his being does not depend upon his coat. The fear of death lasts only so long as man has not realized that his real being does not depend upon his body.

The joy, therefore, of the one who experiences the inner life is beyond comparison greater than that of the average man living only as a captive in his mortal body. Yet the inner life does not necessitate man's adopting a certain way of living, or living an ascetic or a religious life. Whatever his outer occupation may be, it does not matter; the man who lives the inner life lives it through all. Man always looks for a spiritual person in a religious person, or perhaps in what he calls a good person, or in someone with a philosophical mind, but that is not necessarily the case. A person may be religious, even philosophical, he may be religious and good, and yet he may not live the inner life.

There is no distinct outward appearance that can prove a person to be living the inner life, except one thing. When a child grows towards youth, you can see in the expression of that child a light beaming out, a certain new consciousness arising, a new knowledge coming that the child has not known before. That is the sign of youth, yet the child does not say so; he cannot say it, and even if he wanted to, he cannot explain it. And yet you can see it from every move-ment that the child makes; from his every expression, you can find that he is realizing life now. So it is with the soul; when the soul begins to realize the life above and beyond this life, it begins to show; and although the man who real-izes this may refrain from purposely showing it, yet from his expression, his movement, his glance, his voice, from every action and from every attitude, the wise can grasp and the others can feel that he is conscious of some mystery.

The inner life is a birth of the soul; as Christ said, unless the soul is born again it cannot enter the kingdom of heaven. Therefore, the realization of the inner life is entering the kingdom of heaven, and this consciousness, when it comes to the human being, shows itself as a new birth, and with this new birth there comes the assurance of everlasting life.

Chapter 27.

THERE IS A SPIRIT OF FREEDOM
HIDDEN WITHIN MAN

*When man grows out of the outward conventionalities,
then the spirit of freedom, which was closed in so far,
becomes manifest.*

As man grows through the inner life, so he feels a freedom
of thought, speech and action, which comes as a natural
course through his spiritual journey. The reason why this
freedom comes and whence it comes can be explained by the
fact that there is a spirit of freedom hidden within man,
covered by outward conventionalities. When man grows out
of the outward conventionalities, then the spirit of freedom,
which was closed in so far, becomes manifest.

The laws given to humanity are given by those far from
such laws, the elder ones. As for children, certain laws, certain rules are necessary, so those who have not yet evolved
to look at life from the higher point of view are fixed under
certain laws that are taught to them as religion; and these are
as necessary for mankind as the rules given to the children

in the home. If there were no rules given, the children would become unruly; but when the children become grown up, then they begin to see for themselves the reason why rules were given to them and the benefit that these rules were to them, then they can make such rules for themselves as suit them best.

The inner life helps a soul to grow up; when the soul evolves from subjection to mastery, then it makes rules for itself. In the East, therefore, no one tries to criticize a spiritual person; no one stands up to judge his action or to accuse him of something the accuser himself calls wrong. For this reason Jesus Christ has said, "Judge not". But this teaching has been given to point out that "judge not" applies to your equal; for the one who is still more advanced no one can judge. When man has the tendency to judge one more advanced than himself, the consequence is that spiritual advancement deteriorates; because however advanced he may be, those who have not yet advanced pull him down. Therefore humanity, instead of going forward, goes backward. What happened in the case of Jesus Christ? He was judged. The liberated soul, the soul that was made free by divine nature, was judged at the court of man. The less advanced men considered themselves sufficiently learned to judge Christ, and not only to judge but to give sentence.

In whatever period of civilization, when the tendency to judge the one who is advanced has shown itself, there has always come a collapse of the whole civilization. Sarmad, a great Sufi saint who lived in Gwalior, was asked by the Emperor Aurangzeb to attend the mosque, for it was against the rules of the time that anyone keep away from the regular prayers, which took place in the mosque of the state. Sarmad, being a man of ecstasy, living every moment of his day and night in union with God, being God–conscious himself, perhaps forgot or refused. A certain time of prayer or a certain place of prayer to him was nothing; every place to him was a place of prayer; every time was a time of prayer; his every breath was a prayer. As he refused to attend prayers, he was beheaded for breaking the rules that were made for everyone. The consequence was that the Moghul Empire declined, and its downfall can be dated from that time; the entire Moghul civilization, unique in its period, fell to pieces.

The Hindus have always known this philosophy, for the reason that they had a perfect religion, a religion in which one aspect of God was characterized as human; their various devas are nothing but various characteristics of human nature, each of them adored and worshipped. In this way not only God but the whole human nature in all its aspects was adored and worshipped. It is this that makes the Hindu religion perfect. When people say, "This place is sacred, and that other place is not sacred; that particular thing is holy, and all other things not holy," in this way they divide life into many pieces—the life that is one, the life that cannot be divided.

Therefore those who rise above the ordinary conventionalities of life by their inner development come to another consciousness. For them worldly laws are the laws for the children. Those who begin to see this difference between the laws they set before themselves and the laws that are observed by mankind, at first sometimes condemn and then disregard the common laws. They criticize them, and ask, "What is it all for?" But those who come to the fuller realization of the inner laws show respect even for the laws of the children knowing that they *are* the laws for the children and not for the grown-ups, yet they respect them, for they know that it cannot be otherwise. The laws they know can manifest to the one whose soul rises to that realization; but before that soul rises it must have some law by which to live in harmony. Therefore advanced souls regard such laws with respect, and observe them when they are in the community. They do not condemn them; they will not criticize them. They realize that harmony is the principal thing in life, and that we cannot be happy through life if we cannot harmonize with all those around us. Whatever be our grade of evolution, whatever be our outlook on life, and whatever be our freedom, we must have regard for the laws of the majority.

Now the question is, do those who are spiritually advanced have any special conception of morals? Indeed they have; and their morals are great morals, much greater than the average human being can conceive. It is not that by becoming free spiritually from the laws of the generality, they become free from their own laws. They have their own laws to bind them; and these are much higher and much greater laws. No doubt their way of looking at things may be criticized and may not be generally understood. Yet their law is more akin to nature; their laws are in harmony with the spirit. Their laws have their effect as phenomena. And by regarding two morals that are contrary to each other, the morals of the generality and their own morals, they arrive at a plane and a condition where their hands and feet are nailed. That is the symbolical meaning of the nailing of Christ to the cross.

Chapter 28.

THE SINGER OF THE DIVINE SONG, THE ASTROLOGER OF THE ENTIRE COSMOS

> *The eye of the seer becomes a sword that cuts open, so to speak, all things, including the hearts of men, and sees clearly through all they contain.*

Those who live the inner life begin to see a law that is hidden from the average man. There is the law of nature, which is known as science, and that of life, which is called moral law; but beyond science and morals there is another law. It may be called occult law, or in other words inner law; a law that can be understood by an open heart and an awakened soul.

This law manifests to the view of the seer in many and varied forms; sometimes it appears in a quite contrary form to the effect that it has later on in its manifestation. The eye of the seer becomes a sword that cuts open, so to speak, all things, including the hearts of men, and sees clearly through all they contain; but it is a cutting open that is at the same time healing.

In the Qur'an it is said, "He who taught with the pen, taught man that which he knew not." And what does that mean? It means that to the man who lives the inner life, everything that he sees becomes a written character and this whole visible world a book. He reads it as plainly as a letter written by his friend. And besides this, he hears a voice within fhat becomes to him a language. It is an inner language; its words are not the same as the words of the external language. It is a divine language. It is a language without words, which can only be called a voice, and yet it serves as a language. It is like music, which is as clear as a language to the musician. Another person enjoys music, but only the musician knows exactly what it says, what every note is, how it is expressed and what it reveals. Every phrase of music to him has a meaning; every piece of music is a picture to him. But this is so only with a real musician.

Some people profess to have clairvoyance and clairaudience, and very often delude others by giving false prophecies; but the one who lives the inner life does not need to prophesy; he does not need to tell others what he sees and what he hears. It is not only that he is not inclined to do so, but also that he sees no necessity for it; besides, he cannot fully express himself. How difficult it is to translate fully the poetry of one language into the poetry of another! Yet it is only interpreting the ideas of one part of the earth to the people of another part of the same earth. How much more difficult, then, it must be to translate or to interpret the ideas of the divine world to the human world! In what words can they be given? What phrases can be used for them? And after being given even in words and phrases, who would understand them? It is the language of a different world.

Therefore, when the prophets and seers of all ages have given to humanity a certain message and law, it was only the giving of a drop from the ocean they received into their hearts. And this also is a great difficulty, for even this drop is not intelligible. Does every Christian understand the Bible? Does every Muslim know the Qur'an or every Hindu the Vedas? No, they may know the words of the verses, but not always the real meaning. Among the Muslims there are some who know the whole Qur'an by heart, but that does not fulfill the purpose. The whole of nature is a secret book, yet it is an open book to the seer. How can man translate it? How can man interpret it? It is like trying to bring the sea on to the land; one can bring it, but how much?

The understanding of his law gives quite a different outlook on life to the seer; it makes him more inclined to appreciate all that is good and beautiful, to admire all that is worth admiring, to enjoy all that is worth enjoying, to experience all that is worth experiencing. It awakens the sympathy of the seer to love, to tolerate, to forgive, to endure, and to sympathize; it gives the inclination to support, to protect, and to serve those in need. But can he say what he really feels, how he really feels? No, he cannot say it even for himself.

Therefore the one who lives the inner life is all things; he is as a physician who knows things that a physician cannot know; an astrologer who knows much more than the astrologer; an artist who knows that which an artist could not know; a musician who knows what a musician does not know; a poet who knows what the poet cannot perceive. For he becomes the artist of the entire world, the singer of the divine song; he becomes an astrologer of the entire cosmos, which is hidden from the sight of men. He does not need outer things as the signs of knowing the eternal life. His very life is the evidence of the everlasting life. To him death is a shadow; it is a change; it is turning the face from one side to the other. To him all things have their meaning, every movement in this world: the movement of the water, of the air, of the lightning and the thunder and the wind. Every movement has a message for him, it brings to him some sign. To another person it is only the thunder, it is only a storm, but to him every movement has its meaning. And when he rises in his development, not only has every movement its meaning, but in and above every movement there is his command. It is that part of his life that brings him mastery. Besides this, in all affairs of this world, of individuals and multitudes, which confuse people, which bring them despair and cause them depression, which give joy and pleasure, which amuse them, he sees through all. He knows why it comes, whence it comes, what is behind it, what is the cause of it, and behind the seeming cause what is the hidden cause; and if he wished to trace the cause behind the cause he could trace back to the primal cause, for the inner life is lived by living with the primal cause, by being in unity with the primal cause. Therefore the one who lives the inner life, who, in other words, lives the life of God, God is in him and he is in God.

Chapter 29.

SO THE WISE LIVE AMONG ALL THE PEOPLE OF THIS WORLD

The task to be accomplished is the entire forgetting of oneself and harmonizing with one's fellow man.

The position of the person living the inner life becomes like that of a grownup living among many children. At the same time, there seems outwardly no such difference as is apparent in the ages of the children and the grown person, because the difference lies in the size of his outlook, which is not always apparent. One who lives the inner life becomes much older than those around him, and yet outwardly he is the same as every other person. Therefore the man who has arrived at the fullness of the inner life adopts quite a different policy from the one who is just beginning to tread that path, and also a different one from that of the man who knows intellectually something about the inner life, but who does not really live it. The action again is different in the world, for the latter person will criticize others who do not know what he thinks he knows, and will look upon them with pride and conceit, or with contempt, thinking that they have not risen to the mystery, to the height, to which he has risen, and which he understands. He wishes to disconnect himself from people, saying that they are backward in their evolution, and that he cannot go with them. He says, "I am more advanced; I cannot join them in anything; they are different, I am different." He laughs at the petty ideas of those who surround him, and looks upon them as human beings with whom he must not associate, with whom he must not join in all the things they do, because he is much more advanced than they are.

But for the one who comes to the fullness of the inner life it is a great joy to mingle with his fellow man, just as it is for parents to play with their little children. The best moments of their lives are when they feel as a child with their children and when they can join in their play. Parents who are kind and loving, if a child brings them a doll's cup, will pretend that they are drinking tea, and that they are enjoying it; they do not let the child think they are superior, or that this is something in which they must not join. They play with the child, and they are happy with it, because the happiness of the children is theirs also. That is the action of the man who lives the inner life, and it is for this reason that he agrees and harmonizes with people of all grades of evolution, whatever be their ideas, their thoughts, their belief, or their faith; in whatever form they worship or show their religious enthusiasm. He does not say, "I am much more advanced than you are, and to join you would be going backward." The one who has gone so far forward can never go backward, but by joining them he takes them along with him, onward. If he went on alone he would consider that he avoided his duty towards his fellow man, which he should perform. It is the empty pitcher that makes a noise when you knock upon it, but the pitcher that is full of water does not make any sound; it is silent, speechless.

So the wise live among all the people of this world, and they are not unhappy. The one who loves all is not unhappy.

Unhappy is he who looks with contempt at the world, who hates human beings and thinks he is superior to them; the one who loves them thinks only that they are going through the same process that he has gone through. It is from the darkness that he has to come into the light. It is just a difference of moments; and he, with great patience, passes those moments while his fellow men are still in darkness, not making them know that they are in darkness, not letting them feel hurt about it, not looking upon them with contempt, but only thinking that for every soul there is childhood, there is youth and maturity. So it is natural for every human being to go through this process. I have seen with my own eyes souls who have attained saintliness and who have reached to great perfection; and yet such a soul will stand before an idol of stone with another, with a fellow man, and worship, not letting him know that he is in any way more advanced than other men, keeping himself in a humble guise and not making any pretence that he has gone further in his spiritual evolution.

The further such souls go, the more humble they become; the greater the mystery they have realized, the less they speak about it. You would scarcely believe it if I were to tell you that during four years in the presence of my Murshid, hardly more than once or twice did I have a conversation on spiritual matters. Usually the conversation was on worldly things, like everybody else's; nobody would perceive that here was a God-realized man, who was always absorbed in God. His conversation was like that of every other person; he spoke on everything belonging to this world; there was never a spiritual conversation, nor any special show of piety or spirituality, and yet his atmosphere, the voice of his soul, and his presence revealed all that was hidden in his heart.

Those who are God-realized and those who have touched wisdom speak very little on the subject. It is those who do not know who try to discuss it, not because they know but because they themselves have doubts. When there is knowledge, there is satisfaction, there is no tendency towards dispute. When one disputes, it is because there is something not satisfied. There is nothing in this world—wealth, rank, position, power, or learning—that can give such conceit as the slightest little amount of spiritual knowledge; and once a person has that conceit, then he cannot take a further step, he is nailed down to that place where he stands; because the very idea of spiritual realization is in selflessness. Man has either to realize himself as something or as nothing. In the realization of nothingness there is spirituality. If one has any little knowledge of the inner laws of nature and is proud of it, or if one has any sense of thinking, "How good I am, how kind I am, how generous, how well-mannered, how influential, or how attractive," the slightest idea of anything of this kind coming into the mind closes the doors that lead into the spiritual world. It is such an easy path to tread, and yet so difficult. Pride is most natural to a human being. Man may deny a virtue a thousand times in words, but he cannot help admitting it with his feelings, for the ego itself is pride. Pride *is* the ego; man cannot live without it. In order to attain to spiritual knowledge, in order to become conscious of the inner life, a person does not need to learn very much, because here he has to know what he already knows; only he has to discover it himself. For his understanding of spiritual knowledge he does not need the knowledge of anything except himself. He acquires the knowledge of the self that is himself, so near and yet so far.

Another thing the lover of God shows is the same tendency as the human lover's: he does not talk about his love to anybody; he cannot talk about it. Man cannot say how much he loves his beloved; no words can express it; and, besides, he does not feel like talking about it to anybody. Even if he could, in the presence of his beloved he would close his lips. How then could the lover of God make the profession, "I love God"? The true lover of God keeps his love silently hidden in his heart, like a seed sown in the ground; and if the seedling grows, it grows in his actions towards his fellow man. He cannot act except with kindness, he cannot feel anything but forgiveness; every movement he makes, everything he does, speaks of his love, but not his lips.

This shows that in the inner life the greatest principle that one should observe is to be unassuming and quiet, without any show of wisdom, without any manifestation of learning, without any desire to let anyone know how far one has gone. The task to be accomplished is the entire forgetting of oneself and harmonizing with one's fellow man; acting in agreement with all, meeting everyone on his own plane, speaking to everyone in his own tongue, answering the laughter of one's friends with a smile and the pain of another with tears, standing by one's friends in their joy and their sorrow, whatever be one's own grade of evolution. If a man through his life became like an angel, he would accomplish very little; the accomplishment that is most desirable for man is to fulfill the obligations of human life.

Chapter 30.

A LIVING GOD

The goal of the spiritual person is self-realization, and his journey is towards the depth of his own being, his God, his ideal.

Is it power that is the object of the spiritual person, or is it inspiration after which he seeks? It is, in fact, neither of these things that he pursues, but all such things as power and inspiration follow him as he proceeds on his path towards the spiritual goal. The goal of the spiritual person is self-realization, and his journey is towards the depth of his own being, his God, his ideal.

Does such a person sacrifice all interests in life, or does he consider the different objects that people have in their lives as something that leads them astray? Not at all. No doubt his object is the highest that any soul can have, but all other objects he sees before himself in life do not necessarily hinder him on his path; they become as a staircase on his way, making his path easy to tread. Therefore, the person living the inner life never condemns and does not criticize the objects of another, however small or ridiculous they may appear, for he knows that every object in the life of a person is but a stepping stone, which leads him forward if he only wishes to go forward.

There is a time in the life of a soul when it has the desire to play wth dolls; there is a seeking after toys. From the spiritual point of view there is not harm in that, and man sees in time the way that leads to the goal; these are only passing interests leading to others, and in this way man goes forward.

Therefore, according to the view of the seer, man places before himself at different times such objects as riches, pleasure, or a material heaven; the spiritual person starts his journey from the point where these end. The process of evolution is not a straight way, it is more like a wheel that is ever turning. So the experience of the person who treads the spiritual path begins to show a downward tendency, and from that again upwards. For instance, in the spiritual path a person goes backwards: he experiences youth again, for spirituality gives health to the mind and to the body, it being the real life. He experiences vigor, strength, aspiration, enthusiasm, energy, and a living spirit that makes him feel youthful, whatever be his age. Then he becomes as a little child, eager to play, ready to laugh, happy among children; he shows in his personality childlike traits, especially that look one sees in children, where there is no worry, anxiety, or bitter feeling against anyone, where there is a desire to be friendly with all, where there is no pride or conceit, but instead, readiness to associate with anybody, whatever be his class or caste, nation or race. So the spiritual person becomes like a child. The tendency to tears, the readiness for laughter, all these are found in the spiritual person.

As the spiritual person goes further, he shows in his nature infancy. This can be perceived in his innocence. His heart may be lighted with wisdom, yet he is innocent; he is easily deceived, even knowingly, besides being happy under all conditions, like an infant. As the infant has no regard for honor or for insult, neither has the spiritual person. When he arrives at this stage, he answers insult with a smile. Honors given to him are like honors given to a little baby, who does not know to whom they are offered. Only the person who has given the honors knows that they have been given to somebody. The spiritual one is not conscious of it, nor happy in it, nor proud of it. It is nothing to him. The one who has honored him has honored himself, since to the baby it is nothing if somebody should speak in favor of him or against him; the baby does not mind, he is ready to smile at both; so is the spiritual soul.

As the spiritual soul proceeds further he begins to show the real traits of humanity, for there humanity really begins. One can see in such a soul the signs that are the pure characteristics of the human being, devoid of the animal traits. For instance, there is a tendency in him to appreciate every little good deed done by anyone, to admire good wherever he sees it in any person; a tendency to sympathize, whatever be the condition of the person, saint or sinner; a tendency to take interest in the affairs of his friends when called upon to do so; a tendency to sacrifice, not considering what he sacrifices, as long as he is moved to do that action. Respect, gratitude, sincerity, faithfulness, patience, endurance, all these qualities begin to show in the character of that man. It is in this stage that truly he can judge, for at this stage the sense of justice awakens.

But as he grows he continues also to grow backward. He now shows the signs of the animal kingdom; for instance, such a quality as that of the elephant, which, with all its strength and power of giant bulk, is ready to take the load put upon it; the horse, which is ready to serve the rider; and the cow, which lives in the world harmoniously, comes home without being driven, and gives milk that is the right of her calf. These qualities come to the spiritual person. The same thing is taught by Christ.

When he goes on further still there develops in him the quality of the vegetable kingdom, of the plants that bring forth fruit and flowers patiently waiting for the rain from above, and never asking any return from those who come to gather flowers and fruit, giving and never expecting a return, desiring only to bring forth beauty according to the capability that is hidden in them, and letting it be taken by the worthy or unworthy, whoever it may be, without any expectation of appreciation or thanks.

And when the spiritual person advances still further he arrives at the stage of the mineral kingdom. He becomes as a rock—a rock for others to lean on, to depend upon; a rock that stands unmoved amidst the constantly-moving waves of the sea of life; a rock to endure all things of this world whose influence has a jarring effect upon sensitive human beings; a rock of constancy in friendship, of steadfastness in love, of loyalty to every ideal for which he has taken his stand. One can depend upon him through life and death, here and hereafter. In this world where nothing is dependable, which is full of changes every moment, such a soul has arrived at the stage where he shows through all these changes that rock-like quality, proving thereby his advancement to the mineral kingdom.

His further advancement is into the djinn quality, which represents the all-knowing, all-understanding. There is nothing he cannot understand; however difficult the situation, however subtle the problem, whatever be the condition of those around him, he understands it all. A person may come to him hardened with faults that he has committed all his life, and before this understanding that person melts, for whether it be a friend or an enemy, the spiritual soul understands both. Not only has he the knowledge of human nature, but of objects as well and of conditions of life in general in all its aspects.

And when he advances still further, his nature develops into that of an angel. The nature of the angel is to be worshipful. He therefore worships God in all creatures; he does not feel to be any greater or better or any more spiritual himself than anybody else. In this realization he is the worshipper of all the names and forms there are, for he considers them all the names and forms of God. There is no one, however degenerate or looked down upon by the world, who is any less in his eyes. In his eyes there is no one but the divine Being, and in this way every moment of his life is devoted to worship. For him it is no longer necessary that he must worship God at a certain time, or in a certain house, or in a certain manner. There is not one moment that he is not in worship. Every moment of his life he is in worship, he is before God; and being before God at every moment of his life, he becomes so purified that his heart becomes a crystal where everything is clear. Everything is reflected there; no one can hide his thoughts from him, nothing is hidden from him; all is known as clearly as it is known to the other person, and more so. For every person knows his own condition and yet not the reason, but the spiritual being at this stage knows the condition of the person and the reason behind it. Therefore he knows more about every person than that person knows himself.

It is in this stage that his progress culminates and comes to its fullness; and Christ has spoken concerning this in the words: "Be ye perfect, as your Father in heaven is perfect." When that stage arrives, it is beyond all expression. It is a sense, it is a realization, it is a feeling that words can never explain. There is only one thing that can be said and that is that when a person has touched that stage that is called perfection, his thought, speech, and action, his atmosphere, everything becomes productive of God; he spreads God everywhere. Even if he did not speak, still he would spread God; if he did not do anything, still he would bring God. And thus God-realized ones bring to the world the living God. At present there exists in the world only a belief in God; God exists in imagination, in the ideal. It is such a soul, as that of the God-realized ones, which has touched divine perfection, that brings to the earth a living God, who without him would remain only in the heavens.

Chapter 31.

FIVE DIFFERENT KINDS OF SPIRITUAL SOULS

There is no end to the variety of outward appearance of spiritual souls in life; but at the same time, there is no better way of living in this world and yet living the inner life than being oneself both outwardly and inwardly.

Those who live the inner life have to adopt a certain outer form of living in the world amidst people of all kinds. There are five principal ways known that the spiritual souls adopt to live life in the world, although there are many more ways. Very often these souls are found in such forms of life that one could never imagine for one moment that they were living the inner life. It is for this reason that the wise of all ages have taught respect for every human being, whatever be his outward character, and have advised man to think who is beneath that garb, and what it is.

Among the five principal characteristics of the spiritual being the first is the religious character. This is he who lives the religious life, the life of an orthodox person, like everybody else, showing no outward trace of a deeper knowledge or wider view, though he realizes it within himself. Outwardly he goes to his temple or his church, like everybody else. He offers his prayers to the deity in the same form as everybody else, reads the scriptures in the same way that everybody else does, receives the sacraments and asks for the benediction of the church in the same way that everybody else does. He shows no difference, no special characteristics outwardly showing him to be spiritually advanced; but at the same time, while others are doing all their religious actions outwardly, he realizes them in his life in reality. Every religious action to him is a symbolical revelation; prayer to him is a meditation; the scripture to him is his reminder, for the holy book refers him to that which he reads in life and in nature. And therefore, while outwardly he is only a religious man like everybody in the world, inwardly he is a spiritual man.

Another aspect of a spiritual man is to be found in the philosophical mind. He may show no trace at all of orthodoxy or piety; he may seem to be quite a man of the world in business, or in the affairs of the worldly life. He takes all things smoothly, he tolerates all things, endures all things. He takes life easily with his understanding. He understands all things inwardly; outwardly he acts according to life's demand. No one may ever think that he is living the inner life. He may be settling a business affair, and yet he may have the realization of God and truth at the same time. He may not appear at all meditative or contemplative, and yet every moment of his life may be devoted to contemplation. He may take his occupation in everyday life as a means of spiritual realization. No one outwardly may consider for one moment that he is spiritually so highly evolved, except that those who come in contact with him may in time be convinced that he is an honest person, that he is fair and just in his principles and life, and that he is sincere. That is all the religion he needs. In this way his outward life becomes his religion, and his inner realization his spirituality.

The third form of a spiritual being is that of a server, one who does good to others. In this form there may be saints hidden. They never speak about spirituality, nor much about the philosophy of life. Their philosophy and religion are in their action. There is love gushing forth from their heart every moment of their lives, and they are occupied in doing good to others. They consider everyone who comes near them as their brother or sister, as their child; they take an interest in the joy and the sorrow of all people, and do all they can to guide them, to instruct them, to advise them through their lives. In this form the spiritual person may be a teacher, a preacher, or a philanthropist; but in whatever form he may appear, the chief thing in his life is serving mankind, doing good to another, bringing happiness to someone in some form; and the joy that rises from this is high spiritual ecstasy, for every act of goodness and kindness has a particular joy that brings the air of heaven. When a person is all the time occupied doing good to others, there is a constant joy arising; and that joy creates a heavenly atmosphere, creating within him that heaven that is his inner life. This world is so full of thorns, so full of troubles, pains, and sorrows, and in this same world he lives; but by the very fact of his trying to remove the thorns from the path of another, although they prick his own hands, he rises, and this gives him that inner joy that is his spiritual realization.

There is the fourth form of a spiritual person, which is the mystic form; and that form is difficult to understand, because the mystic is born. Mysticism is not a thing that is learned; it is a temperament. A mystic may have his face turned towards the north while he is looking towards the south; a mystic may have his head bent low and yet he may be looking up; his eyes may be open outwardly while he may be looking inwardly; his eyes may be closed and yet he may be looking outwardly. The average man cannot understand the mystic, and therefore people are always at a loss when dealing with him. His "yes" is not the same "yes" that everybody says; his "no" has not the same meaning as that which everybody understands. In almost every phrase he says there is some symbolical meaning. His every outward action has an inner signficance. A man who does not understand his symbolical meaning may be bewildered by hearing a phrase that is nothing but confusion to him.

A mystic may take one step outwardly, while inwardly he has taken a thousand; he may be in one city, and may be working in another place at the same time. A mystic is a phenomenon in himself and a confusion to those around him. He himself cannot tell them what he is doing, nor will they understand the real secret of the mystic. For this is someone who is living the inner life, and at the same time covering that inner life by outer action; his word or movement is nothing but the cover of some inner action. Therefore those who understand the mystic never dispute with him. When he says, "Go," they go; when he says, "Come," they come; when he comes to them they do not say, "Do not come"; they understand that it is the time when he must come; and when he goes from them they do not ask him to stay, for they know it is the time when he must go.

Neither the laughter of a mystic nor his tears are to be taken as any outward expression that means something. His tears may perhaps be a cover for very great joy; his smile, his laughter may be a cover for a very deep sentiment. His open eyes, his closed eyes, the turning of his face, his glance, his silence, his conversation—none of these has the meaning one is accustomed to attribute to them. Yet the mystic does not do this purposely; he is made thus; no one could purposely do it even if he wished—no one has the power to do it. The truth is that the soul of the mystic is a dancing soul. It has realized that inner law, it has fathomed that mystery for which souls long, and in the joy of that mystery the whole life of the mystic becomes a mystery. You may see the mystic twenty times a day, and twenty times he will have a different expression. Every time his mood is different, and yet his outward mood may not at all be his inner mood. The mystic is an example of God's mystery in the form of man.

The fifth form in which a person who lives the inner life

appears is a strange form, a form very few people can under-stand. He puts on the mask of innocence outwardly to such an extent that those who do not understand may easily consider him unbalanced, peculiar, or strange. He does not mind about it, for the reason that it is only his shield. If he were to admit before humanity the power that he has, thou-sands of people would go after him, and he would not have one moment to live his inner life. The enormous power that he possesses governs inwardly lands and countries, control-ling them and keeping them safe from disasters such as floods and plagues, and also wars; keeping harmony in the country or in the place in which he lives; and all this is done by his silence, by his constant realization of the inner life. To a person who lacks deep insight he will seem a strange being. In the language of the East he is called *majdhub*. That same idea was known to the ancient Greeks and traces of it are still in existence in some places, but mostly in the East. There are souls to be found today in the East, living in this garb of a self-realized man who shows no trace outwardly of philosophy or mysticism or religion, or any particular morals; and yet his presence is a battery of power, his glance most inspiring; there is a commanding expression in his looks, and if he ever speaks, his word is the promise of God. What he says is truth, but he rarely speaks a word. It is difficult to get a word out of him, but once he has spoken, what he says is done.

There is no end to the variety of the outward appearance of spiritual souls in life; but at the same time there is no better way of living in this world and yet living the inner life than being *oneself,* outwardly and inwardly. Whatever be one's profession, work, or part in the outer life, one can perform it sincerely and truthfully and fulfill one's mission in the outer life thoroughly, at the same time keeping the inner realization that the outer life, whatever be one's occu-pation, should reflect the inner realization of truth.

Chapter 32.

"I AM THE WAY AND THE TRUTH"

*I went among the pious and the godly and was so often
deceived; and I went among those who were looked down
upon by others and among them I found real souls.*
— a Persian Sufi

The maturity of the soul may be pictured as the moment
when a little girl, beginning to grow up, no longer gives the
same importance and attention to her dolls: her sentiments
and her desires have changed. It does not mean that she did
not have love or sentiment before; she had those; but with
maturity her consciousness developed, and the result of that
development was that all the toys and dolls and the various
things that she used to pay so much attention to did not
matter any more.

This maturity does not depend upon a certain age, but it
does depend upon certain surroundings; it is just like a fruit
that ripens when put in a warm place. Environment helps
the maturing of the soul; nevertheless the ideal is that the
fruit should ripen on the tree, for that is the place for fruit

195

to ripen. All the different attempts to make the soul ripen may help, though it is like fruit that is no longer on the tree but has been put in some warm place.

There are people who think that by renouncing the world one will arrive at the maturity of the soul. There are others who think it can be achieved by inflicting all kinds of torments and suffering upon oneself. Often people have asked me if some kind of suffering, some kind of torture, would help to mature their soul. I told them that if they wanted to torture themselves I could tell them a thousand ways, or they might themselves think of a thousand things, but that as far as I knew there was no necessity for it. If one wants to torture oneself for the sake of torture one may do so, but not for spiritual perfection.

As fruit ripens in the course of nature, so it is in the course of nature that the soul should mature; and it is no use being disappointed or disheartened about ourselves and about those near and dear to us, worrying because our husband, wife, father, or mother does not look at spiritual matters in the same way as we do. In the first place no man, however wise or pious, has the right to judge another soul. Who knows what is hidden behind every action, appearance, speech, and manner? No one. And when a person begins to know what is hidden in the human soul, in spite of all deluding appearances he will have respect, a respect for mankind, as he realizes that in the depth of every soul is He whom one worships.

No one knows what is a person's inner religion, his inner conception. And one will find many true souls whose heart is enclosed in a kind of hard shell; no one knows that the very essence of God is in their heart, as the outer shell is so hard that no one can understand it. That is why a Sufi from Persia said, "I went among the pious and the godly and was so often deceived; and I went among those who were looked down upon by others and among them I found real souls." It is easy to blame, it is easy to look down upon someone, but it is difficult really to know how deep someone's soul is.

No doubt there are signs of maturity, but who knows them, and how does one recognize them? The signs of maturity are like the subtlety one sees between youthful lovers. For the soul to mature a passion must have awakened it—a passion for the incomprehensible, for that which is the longing of every soul.

Life on earth is just like Gulliver's travels, where all the people seem to belong to a different world, to be of a different size. Before the traveller there are numberless little children, and before him there appear many drunken people, drunken souls. There is a saying of the Prophet Muhammad that there will appear in the hereafter, on the Day of Judgment, a being in the form of a witch, and man will be frightened at the sight of this witch and will cry out, "O Lord, what a horrible sight is this! Who is this?" And he will receive the answer from the angels, "This is the same world, the world that attracted you throughout your life, which you have worshipped, adored, and esteemed as most valuable, and which was all you desired. This is the same world that is before you." All people's desires, whether they concern wealth, rank, possession, positon, honor, or pleasure, all these fade away with the maturity of the soul. All claims to love such as "I am your brother, or your sister, or your son, or your daughter," mean very little to the mature soul. A mature soul does not need to wait for the day in the hereafter when he sees the world in the form of a witch; he sees it now. No sooner has the soul matured than he sees the unreality of the world that man has always considered real, and all such words that one uses in everyday language become meaningless.

All distinctions and differences, such as sect and creed and community, mean little to the soul who has awakened. The experience of the mature soul is like the experience of the man who watched a play performed on the stage at night, and in the morning he saw the same stage in the sun and saw that all the palaces and gardens and the actor's costumes were unreal.

When a soul has arrived at this stage, at this maturity, what happens? It is the same as when a person grows up: he takes either the right way or the wrong way. His reaction to this realization of life has three aspects. One reaction is that in answer to every claim of love and attention and respect, he says, "Oh, no! I don't believe you, I have had enough. I understand what your claims are. I don't belong to you. I won't listen!" About that which attracts him he thinks, "You are a temptation. Go away, leave me. I want to be alone. I know what you are." And by this he becomes more and more indifferent to the world and isolated in the crowd. He feels solitary; he goes to the cave in the mountain or into the forest; he retires from the world and lives the life of an ascetic, at war with the world although at peace with God.

There is another aspect of this reaction, which is that a man who understands the reality of all things becomes more sympathetic to his fellow men. It is this man who out of sympathy sacrifices his love for solitude, his love for being exclusive, and goes into the crowd among those who do not understand him, continually trying to understand them from morning until evening. And the more he advances on this path, the more he develops love. He mourns over the unreality and the falsehood of life, but at the same time he is there in the midst of it. His work is to help those who may be disappointed at the results of all the little expectations they had of their love and devotion. For such people every disappointment, every heartbreak, is a surprise, a shock, something that suddenly comes upon them, while for him it is normal, it is the nature of life. He stands beside the disappointed ones, he comforts them, he strengthens them. In the realm of religion, for instance, if he happens to be among those who have a certain belief or dogma, he may be above it, but he will stand beside them in that particular belief or dogma; he does not consider that he is different or above them. If he happens to be in business, in some industry, or in worldly affairs, although he does not aim at any profit, he stands with the others in order to keep harmony.

He will even sacrifice his life in this way, and he enjoys doing all things while caring nothing for them.

This is the manner of an actor on the stage. If he is made a king he is not very proud of his kingship; if he is made a servant he is not impressed by that, for he knows and understands that in his king's robe or servant's livery, he is neither a king nor a servant; he is himself. In reality it is such souls who come to save the world. They are like the elder brothers of humanity who help the younger. To them there is no feeling of position, title, or spiritual grade. They are one with all and they take part in the pain and joy of all.

But then there is a third reaction upon a soul, and that is the thought, "If all that I touch, all that I see, and all that I perceive are unreal, I must find out as best I can what is real." Such a person is a warrior, for he has a battle before him to fight. And what is this battle? It is seeking after the truth. It is just like a person who is swimming: at every stroke he advances, yet at every effort he makes in going forward, the waves come to push him back. In the same way, life is a continual struggle for the seeker for truth.

Even in things that might seem to be covering the truth the seeker may be deluded, for there is a very important thing that he has to consider. Christ has said, "I am the way and the truth." This shows that there are two things: there is the way and there is the truth. The way may lead a person to the goal, but the way may also become like a maze to him. It shows how careful one has to be, that even on the way that seems to lead to the truth one may become puzzled. For in reality life is a maze, a continual puzzle, and it is for love of the puzzle that man goes into it; even a seeker after truth does so, as it is his nature to go into the maze first. If a knower of truth were to call a seeker and tell him, "Here is the truth," he would say, "This is something unheard of! Truth at the first step! How is it possible? It should be many years before I can arrive at it. One life is not sufficient, I must live a thousand lives in order to realize the truth!" But verily, for the lover of the puzzle, even a thousand lives are not enough. Besides, every man is not ready to accept the bare truth; he is not accustomed to it. On hearing the truth he says, "It is too simple. I want something that I cannot understand."

In point of fact truth is simple; it is man who makes it difficult for himself. He has to get all other aspects of knowledge from outside, but truth is something that is within himself. It is something that is nearest to us though we imagine it to be farthest; it is something that is within, though we imagine it to be outside; it is knowledge itself we want to acquire. Thus the seeker is engaged in a continual struggle: struggle with himself, stuggle with others, and struggle with life. And at the end of the journey he always finds that he has travelled because it was his destiny to travel, and he discovers that his starting point is the same as his final goal.

Chapter 33.

THE DANCE OF THE SOUL

I passed into nothingness, I vanished; and lo! I was all living. — Abu Yazid al-Bistami

We see in the life of an infant that there comes a moment when it smiles to itself and moves its little feet and legs as if dancing, bringing delight to the one who looks on and creating life in the atmosphere. What is it that suddenly springs into being in the heart of the infant, ignorant of the pains and pleasures of life, that gives expression to its eyes, that inspires its movements and voice? In ancient times people said, "This is the spirit coming;" they thought it was an angel or fairy speaking to the child. But in reality it is the soul, which at that moment rises in ecstasy, making all things dance. There are many delightful experiences in life, but joy is something greater and deeper than delight; it springs from the innermost being, and there can be no better description of the spring of joy than the dance of the soul.

One finds in the life of every person, sorrowful or happy, wise or foolish, moments when he begins to sing or move.

Joy may be expressed by a smile, it may even be expressed in tears, but in all it is the dance of the soul. This heavenly bliss is not only for mankind; it comes to all beings. Man lives his life in an artificial world and seldom has a chance to see the beauty of nature; this ecstasy is to be found in the forests, in the wilderness where the great yogis, sages, saints, seers, and prophets received their inspiration. One can see it in what is called in the East the dance of the peacocks— the peacocks expressing the impulse of joy, inspired and blessed by the sublime beauty around them. Birds and animals all have their moments of joy, and one can hear this in their voices and in their song, but its greatest expression is in their dance. To nearly all animals there come moments when the blessing of heaven descends upon them, and they respond by dancing.

This blessing is revealed in every aspect of life, even in inanimate objects such as trees and plants; even there we see in the spring the rising of life. Flowers and plants are but different expressions of the one life, the source of all harmony, beauty, and joy. Someone asked the Prophet for a definition of the soul, and he answered in one sentence, "The soul is an action of God." Nothing could be more expressive. Thus joy is the action of the inner or divine life, and when it shows itself in any form it is the reaction to the action of God. It is this that may be called the dance of the soul, and it has inspired all the great musicians and poets. Why do the music of Wagner, of Beethoven and the words of Shakespeare live so long, and continually give new joy and inspiration? Why has not all music and poetry the same effect? Because poetry is one thing, and the dance of the soul another. The dance of the soul is beyond mere poetry, and when music expresses itself as the dance of the soul it becomes something higher than music. Man is accustomed to external knowledge, wanting to learn and understand this thing and that, but beauty does not come so naturally, because beauty is beyond all knowledge; it is intended to prepare man to express his soul.

How often do we confuse these two things: inspiration and education. Education is the preparation for inspiration. Education prepares the mind to be a better means of expression for the natural spring that is to be found in the heart. When education becomes a hobby and inspiration is forgotten, then the soul becomes choked, and where there is no life man is mechanical, unreal; he may write poetry, compose music, and paint pictures, but they will all be lifeless, for he himself is a machine. It is the soul itself that is life, knowledge, and beauty.

Kalidasa was the most learned poet of the Sanskrit age, and yet he had never been educated. The language of Kabir, another poet of India, was most ordinary, and yet when those who attached importance to the delicacy and conventions of Hindi heard his words, they forgot all conventions, for his poetry brought life, it sprang from the soul, it was spirit. His grammar was faulty, but nevertheless his verses made that impression because the words were living, the soul was dancing. The purpose of life is to become more living, to allow the soul to live more; and that is the lesson given by Christ when he tells us to raise our light on high. It means allowing the soul to express itself. It does not matter what our life is, what our pursuit is; in order to fulfill the purpose of life we need not be in a temple or a church. Whatever our life's pursuit, we can be as spiritual as a priest or a clergyman living a life of continual praise. Our work should be our religion, whatever our occupation may be. The soul should express itself in every aspect of life, and then it will surely fulfill its purpose. Life comes naturally to the soul, if only we open ourselves for the spirit to rise.

There is an old story from India that expresses this philosophy. The Hindu heaven or paradise is called Indra-Loka, where the god Indra is king, and where there are *peris,* the angels or fairies whose task is to dance before Indra. There was one fairy from Indra-Loka who descended to earth, and loved an earthly being. By the power of her magic she brought this earthly being to paradise; but when this became known to Indra she was cast out from paradise and the lovers were separated.

This legend is symbolic of the human soul. Originally the peri, who represents the soul, belonged to Indra-Loka, the kingdom of God, the sphere full of peace, joy, and happiness. Life there is nothing but joy; it is a dance. Life and love come from God, and raise every soul until it dances. In its pure condition the soul is joy, and when it is without joy its natural condition is changed; then it depends upon the names and forms of the earth and is deprived of the dance of the soul, and therein lies the whole tragedy of life. The wrath of Indra symbolizes the breach of the law that the highest love must be for God alone. It is natural that the soul is attracted to the spirit and that the true joy of every soul lies in the realization of the divine spirit.

The absence of this realization keeps the soul in despair. In the life of every poet, thinker, artist, or scientist there come moments when ideas or words are given to him; they are given at that time and at no other. This is the moment when unconsciously the soul has an opportunity to breathe. Man does not usually allow his soul to breathe; the portal is closed up in the life of the earth. Man closes it by ignorance; he is absorbed in things of much less importance, so when the door opens and the soul is able to breathe even one breath, it becomes alive in that one single moment, and what emerges is beauty and joy, making man express himself in song or dance. In that way heavenly beauty comes on earth.

The things that catch man's mind are always living things. The poems of Rumi have lived for eight hundred years and they are still living; they bring joy and ecstasy whenever they are sung or recited. They are ever-living life, expressing an everlasting beauty. It is the power of God, and it is a mistake for man ever to presume it to be possible to produce that by study. It is impossible; it is the power of God above that brings out the perfection of beauty. Man can never make the soul dance, but he can make himself a fit instrument for the expression of his soul. The question is, in what way can he do so?

The soul is the spirit of God, and the spirit of God lives within the shrine of the heart; this shrine can be closed or it can be open. There are some things in life that open it, and some that close it. The things that close the heart are those that are contrary to love, tolerance, and forgiveness, such as coldness, bitterness, ill-will, and a strong sense of duality. The world is more disturbed today than ever before; in many ways man seems to be going from bad to worse, and yet he thinks that he is progressing. The problem is not lack of organization or of civilization. Man has both these things; what he lacks is the expression of the soul. He closes his door to his fellow man; he closes the shrine of the heart, and by doing so keeps God away from himself and others. Nation is set against nation, race against race, religion against religion. Therefore, more than ever before there is a need for the realization of this philosophy. It is not that all religions should become one or that all races should become one; that can never be. What is needed is undivided progress, and the making of ourselves into examples of love and tolerance.

It will not come by talking about it, by discussing and arguing, but by self-realization, by making ourselves examples of what we should be, by giving love, accepting love, and showing in our action gentleness, consideration, and the desire for service, for the sake of the God in whom we can all unite beyond the narrow barriers of race and creed.

"I passed into nothingness, I vanished; and lo! I was all living." All who have realized this secret of life understand that life is one, but that it exists in two aspects: first as immortal, all-pervading, and silent life; and secondly as mortal, active, and manifested in variety. The soul, being of the first aspect, becomes deluded, helpless, and captive by experiencing life in contact with the mind and body, which are of the second aspect. The gratification of the desires of the body and the fancies of the mind does not suffice the soul, whose purpose is the experience of its own phenomena in the seen and the unseen, but whose inclination is to be itself and nothing else. When delusion makes it feel that it is helpless, mortal, and captive, it finds itself out of place. This is the tragedy of life that keeps all the strong and the weak, the rich and the poor dissatisfied, constantly looking for something, they do not know what. The Sufi, realizing this, takes the path of annihilation, and by the guidance of a teacher on the path he finds at the end of his journey that the destination was himself.

"I wandered in the pursuit of my own self. I was the traveler, and I am the destination," says Iqbal.

Hazrat Inayat Khan, founder of the Sufi Order in the West, was born in India in 1882. A master of classical Indian music by the age of twenty, he relinquished a brilliant career to devote himself to the spiritual path. In 1910, acting upon the guidance of his teacher, he became one of the first teachers of the Sufi tradition in the West. For a decade and a half he travelled throughout Europe and the United States, giving lectures and guiding an ever-growing group of seekers. In 1926, he returned to India, where he died the following year.

Information about the Sufi Order in the West may be obtained by writing:

Sufi Order National Secretariat
P.O. Box 85569
Seattle, Washington 98145-1569